HOUSTON HAS A PROBLEM!

THE SHOCKING REAL-LIFE STORY OF A SEXUALLY ABUSED CHILD

SAINT ANDREWS

authorHOUSE

AuthorHouse™ UK
1663 Liberty Drive
Bloomington, IN 47403 USA
www.authorhouse.co.uk
Phone: UK TFN: 0800 0148641 (Toll Free inside the UK)
*   UK Local: 02036 956322 (+44 20 3695 6322 from outside the UK)*

Published by AuthorHouse 05/28/2021

ISBN: 978-1-6655-9003-7 (sc)
ISBN: 978-1-6655-9002-0 (e)

Print information available on the last page.

Any people depicted in stock imagery provided by Getty Images are models,
and such images are being used for illustrative purposes only.
Certain stock imagery © Getty Images.

This book is printed on acid-free paper.

INTRODUCTION

"Success is to be measured not so much by the position that one has reached in life as by the obstacles which he has overcome." – Booker T. Washington

My first childhood memory is of my sixteen-year-old chubby white male babysitter molesting me daily. He was the younger brother of the eighteen-year-old slim-build male babysitter who molested my older sister. How long it went on, I honestly don't remember. The year was 1969, and I was four years old. I did not know I was being molested. I figured he liked me, and that's what people did when they liked someone.

The babysitter was always naked from the waist down. He watched TV, and I would fall asleep between his legs, often with his penis in my mouth like a pacifier. This is how I learned the art of pleasing a man. I learned to enjoy putting his penis in my mouth. When he was finished, he always laid me between his legs, and we would both take a nap.

I can still smell him, although I can't remember exactly what he looked like. I only remember his body… chubby, stocky, white. Over time I grew to love and crave his touch and his attention, and I remember feeling a sense of safety and comfort in his arms. This is how I began my journey in life.

Now, I know what you are probably thinking. You're thinking, "Oh, my God, how awful!" And in some ways, you would be right to feel this way, but life is not so simple. One must consider the fundamental truth that everything in the universe is relative.

Did my seemingly tragic beginnings send me down a road of drug and alcohol abuse followed by one broken relationship after another? Did it propel me to pursue my dreams and do things others only dream about? Or did it provide me with the foundation and the authority to write this book so that someday I might help others?

The answer is yes to all the above. Everything in life and in the universe is a place of half-truths and half-lies. There is black, there is white, there is positive energy, and there is negative energy. These polarized extremes are only degrees of the same infinite string and are manifested at the level of creation. Where does hate start and love begin?

So, as you read further, I ask you to let go of your preconceived notions; they will not serve you here. Let me take you into my world and allow you to see the world through my eyes and take a walk in my shoes, after which, you may decide: Does Houston truly have a problem?

CHAPTER 1

GROWING UP TEXAS STYLE

I was born in the mid-sixties during the Chinese year of the snake. Like most of us raised in Western culture, I naturally presumed the snake represented the devil in the garden of Eden. You know the story. The fallen angel took on the form of a snake to deceive poor clueless Eve, who, of course, talked Adam into defying God Almighty. I don't know about you, but if I had the relationship with God that Adam had, I would have just left that apple alone. I mean, why blow a good thing for an apple?

It wasn't until much later that I discovered the snake was actually a globally revered sacred animal and even worshipped by many cultures. Many eastern religions believe snakes are the embodiment of wisdom and knowledge. I like that about the snake's symbol, as I've always had a high sense of curiosity. I like knowing why something works a certain way or why people do the things they do. I guess you might say I've been looking for answers all my life.

When my spirit left eternity and decided to enter this world, my father filled out the birth information, proudly naming me Houston, Jr. Believe it or not, I hated my name for a long time. I wanted to be called Michael. Like Michael Jackson. I remember being quite angry at my father when my mother first told me the story of my christening.

They were quite a couple, my mother and father. They were childhood sweethearts, which to me seemed very romantic and even magical. My mother was 13 when they met, and my father was two years older. They met in the cotton fields of glorious Lubbock, Texas, the home of the Texas Tech Red Raiders, The County Line BBQ restaurant, and Buddy Holly.

My mom kept the house very peaceful and quiet, and no matter where we lived, Mom always made it feel like home. I don't know how she kept everything together. Somehow, we always had more than enough food on the table every night. She cooked, she cleaned, she took care of us, she took us to church every Sunday, and she still found time to work 5-6 days a week at the Navy Exchange.

I've always been the proudest of my mom. She was a beautiful black woman. She was elegant with a genuinely pleasant nature and regal demeanor that people noticed immediately. I remember wanting to be my mom, with her sexy halter tops and big hoop earrings, platform open toe heels and polyester pants. She was simply beautiful inside and out.

My dad was a proud sailor in the United States Navy. Unfortunately, that meant he was out to sea eighty percent of the time while I was growing up. But when he was home, it was party central at our house, that's for sure. My parents always found a good reason to celebrate. In the early days, there were always parties and music wherever we lived.

Music was always playing in the Andrews' residence and still is to this day. My parents were both big fans of all sorts of great soul music like Diana Ross, Sam Cooke, Aretha Franklin, The Jackson Five, and my father's favorite, Marvin Gaye. My dad always played music, either in the house on his LP player or in the car on his 8-track player. Looking back now, I can see my father most influenced my passion for music that would later come full throttle into my life.

My dad didn't really know his mother, and his father wasn't around much either. He and his four brothers were raised in foster homes, but they all went to the same high school. Back in my dad's high school days, his nickname was "Red" because he had light skin and the devil's smile. He was the way-too-cool-for-school type of guy. He was just under six feet tall and a real looker, the ladies would always say about him. He was "a lover, not a fighter," and he was always the life of any party.

I've been told many times I look like my father. The funny thing is, I didn't find my father very attractive as a child. After all, he wasn't white, and I had learned to equate white with attractive and sexy. Regardless of my opinion at the time, my father had a special quality. He had that X-factor everybody loved. Actually, both of my parents were very special people, and they were a perfect match.

Then there was my big sister, who is a year older than me. She was loyal to a fault; maybe even a little too giving and controlling at times. I like to believe it was my sister who got me through some of my worst years as we were growing up. It was also my sister who gave me my childhood nickname, "Bubba." Apparently, at that age, my sister couldn't say "brother." She tried and tried, but what came out of her mouth always sounded like Bubba. After a while, everyone thought the name was cute, and that was that.

In the early 1960s, Lubbock, TX was as racist as one could get in America. Negroes, as we were called back then, lived on the east side, and the white folks lived on the west side, and none of the two met unless one was a maid like my grandmother. She sometimes cooked, and she cleaned white people's homes. She often told me to "never trust a white person because in the end, you are just another nigger to the white man." Maybe it was the way they treated her that made her bitter, or maybe she was just jealous, I don't know.

I remember going to the white people's house to pick up my grandma one day. When we knocked on the front door of the big house, the white lady who answered the door told us we weren't allowed to use the front door. We needed to go around the back and wait in the back yard until my grandmother came outside.

I couldn't blame my grandmother for being bitter or even jealous of the white people she served. Everything was better on the west side. The stores were newer and filled with things we poor black folks could only dream about. And the grass was definitely greener there. They actually had grass, whereas the lawns on the east side were mostly covered with dirt, rocks, and weeds. The streets were bigger, too, and paved. One never saw a pack of stray dogs roaming the streets at night down the white people's neighborhoods like on the east side where one could get rabies from the backs of dogs and wild cats.

But most of all, I remember the people on the west side. They just looked happier than folks on the east side. They were dressed nicely and appeared more confident than the people on the east side.

The white people's homes on the west side were like Hollywood mansions compared to the small single and double shotgun homes on the east side.

Of course, there were a handful of Negroes on the east side who had lovely homes. These would be your black lawyers, doctors, pastors, congressmen, funeral directors, and the lucky few that worked for the state.

However, what the east side lacked in opulent homes, it made up for in cars. Lubbock's east side had more Cadillacs and Lincoln town cars than the west side of town… Crazy, right?

Anyway… Life was simple back then. Everything boiled down to either black or white. In the 1960s America, you knew your place no matter what side of the tracks you lived on. People rarely considered stepping outside of that box, well, at least in the great state of Texas, one sure as hell didn't dare cross certain lines.

CHAPTER 2

MOVING TO CALIFORNIA

I was four years old in 1969 when the Navy moved my family to Hunters Point, California. After leaving Texas and spending a brief stint at the Navy base in Rhode Island, we arrived in California and moved into what looked like round metal huts from an episode of M*A*S*H. The place was one room, like a studio apartment. It was tiny, but I was happy because I was young enough not to know the difference.

I remember my sister and I used to jump up and down on our bed, which was directly in front of one of two windows. I was so young then I can only remember laughing and running around and playing all day near the pier, which was only a few yards in front of our hut. I guess that early experience of living so close to the ocean is why I love the sea. I've always felt the most comfortable by the water. Something about the ocean has always made me want to jump into the water and let the waves carry me away to some distant, magical paradise.

I remember always playing with my sister or going fishing at the dock with my dad. I didn't like watching those poor creatures suffer when my dad would pull them out of the water and onto the pier. I felt sorry for the fish.

Soon after moving to Hunters Point, my father received his housing voucher, and we moved to a small apartment at the Alameda Naval Station housing. No sooner than we moved into the house, my dad was preparing to go overseas for another nine-to-eighteen-month tour of duty: the Vietnam War was in full swing, and duty called.

After my dad left for Vietnam, my mother worked six days a week at the base Navy Exchange. Sometimes my sister and I had to make our own breakfast and dinner. I was a master chef at making fried bologna, grilled cheese sandwiches, and scrambled eggs at an early age.

My sister and I handled being alone pretty well. Our parents gave us strict rules we never crossed. We were good kids and, for the most part, did what we were told without question, except maybe on one occasion. For reasons I can't recall, my sister decided to bake me like a cake. She put me into a huge turkey pot and placed me in the oven. Then she poured a bag of flour over my head, so all you could see were my eyes. I was ready to be roasted. Luckily for me, it was a gas stove, and she didn't know how to light the oven. A few minutes later, my mother's lifelong friend, the woman I call my aunt, stopped by to check on us. And thank God she did! I was literally mere seconds away from being roasted alive.

My sister and I sometimes spent our time playing dress up in my mother's clothes. We put on mom's wigs, and sometimes we put on her makeup and even her jewelry. Another favorite thing we did was watching our favorite TV shows and pretending we were married to the stars. I had a massive childhood crush on William Shatner, who played Captain Kirk on *Star Trek*. I often imagined Captain Kirk taking me in his arms and kissing me, like the famous kiss between him and Lieutenant Uhura, which was the first-ever interracial kiss on network television.

When I wasn't playing games or watching TV with my sister, I enjoyed being by myself. I read anything, newspapers, comics, the back of a cereal box. My passion for reading back then was insatiable. My collection of comic books was massive for a kid my age: I had comic books stacked to the ceiling on one wall. I got all my comics from my dad. Apparently, he spent a lot of his leisure time on the ship reading them. He saved all the comics he had bought during his tour duty in duffle bags and gave them to me every time he returned home.

I would daydream for hours about being magical, having superpowers, and flying through the galaxy in a flying saucer. I was obsessed with a Japanese pre-anime superhero called Ultraman. Ultraman, like most children's shows back then, came on every day after school.

CHAPTER 3

SINS OF THE FATHER

My Dad was kicked out of college after his first year and lost his full scholarship. As it turned out, a white team member threatened him after practice one day over something. My dad responded by threatening to shoot the guy at practice in front of the entire team. Not a good idea in any era. Years later, my dad would tell me that losing his scholarship and having to leave college was his biggest regret.

God bless her, my mom always kept us fed and clothed and gave us lots of love. I felt safe and close to my mother. I often slept in her bed with her when my dad was gone. As for my dad, well, I hardly knew him. He was gone overseas nine months at a time.

Even though I hardly knew my dad, I was utterly terrified of him! Unknowingly, my mother created my fear of my dad. As she didn't like to spank us, her solution was to wait until my father came home and then told him everything my sister and I had done wrong while he was gone. This would result in a series of spankings from my dad for our bad behavior. He'd say, "Go, get my belt" or "You better not make me have to go get it." Another of his favorite taunts was, "I know you are not going to do it again!" He'd say this over and over as he was spanking us with his thick black leather belt! Not surprisingly, my dad's homecomings weren't something I looked forward to in those days. Sometimes I wished he'd never come home.

There were other reasons I feared my dad in those early days. One thing was his drug use. Just like most military men returning from Vietnam, Dad was high from smoking pot all day, every day. His eyes always looked bloodshot like a demon in a horror movie. Sometimes he came home carrying a large brown grocery bag filled with bushels of smelly green grass. He'd go to the living room and pour the grass on our glass coffee table.

My dad became someone else after smoking the green weeds, and I didn't like that version of him at all. Once, he caught me watching him. He looked at me with those blood red devil eyes and started yelling and cursing at me to get back in my room before he whipped my little behind.

My dad's appetite for drugs was only rivaled by his taste for strange women. One time, he brought a lady home while our mother was at work at the Navy Exchange. She had light skin, bright eyes, and a slim waist. She had long, pretty hair, real hair, not a wig, a pair of big, over-the-top disco glasses, and a bright, colorful scarf. She looked like a Soul Train dancer. What I remember most about her was the unmistakable "please like me" look on her face. I can still see her leaning over me, smiling from ear to ear, and handing me a crumpled brown paper bag with a handful of walnuts inside. I didn't like walnuts then, and I don't much care for them now. However, my natural fear of my dad took over, and I politely thanked the "walnut lady" and went outside to the playground.

After about twenty or thirty minutes, I saw my father and the "walnut lady" coming out of the house together. He walked her to her car and then kissed her like he kissed Mommy. I was hurt and confused, and even angry. I knew the Ten Commandments, and I knew what daddy was doing was a sin, but I never told anyone what I saw.

CHAPTER 4

THE BABYSITTER AND ME

My family settled quickly into our new Navy housing. As my father was out to sea again, and my mom worked at the Navy Exchange, she asked our neighbor, a white lady from the apartment next door, if one of her boys could babysit us while she was at work. I must say I feel sorry for my mom; she had no idea her decision would alter my and this family's futures.

Our neighbor had two sons: one was 18 years old, tall and thin with black hair, and the other was chubby, 16 or 17 years old, with dirty blond hair and big blue eyes. Our neighbor told my mom that her older son was willing to look after us. It was 1969, and I was four years old. That was when it all began.

One day, I came in from playing out in front of our apartment. When I entered the living room, I saw my five-year-old sister standing there. The babysitter had my blanket over his lap, and my sister's hand was under the blanket. The babysitter's eyes were closed, so he had not noticed me standing there watching. I could see something was sticking up from under the blanket. I really wanted to see what my sister was playing with. So, being the curious kid I was, I decided to run over and lift the blanket.

The first thing I saw was my sister's little hands holding the babysitter's very erect penis. I could hear him telling her to go up and down faster. I watched in complete fascination. I figured they must be playing a game, and I didn't want to be left out.

At that point, the babysitter opened his eyes and saw me. He didn't stop my sister, but every time I tried to touch his penis, he would get angry and tell me "No" and "Go away." But I couldn't stop looking at it. I remember being hurt and upset that he would let my sister play with it but not me.

Then, before I knew it, the strangest thing happened. Suddenly, he began to moan out loud and told my sister to go faster. And then a minute later, I saw it for the first time: semen. As for my sister, well, she was terrified and ran out of the house. Eventually, he made me leave the room too. As

I left, I carried with me another secret. I would never tell anyone what happened that afternoon.

The skinny babysitter never returned after that day. Looking back, I imagine he was probably worried my sister might tell what happened if he came back around. So, the next day, his chubby brother became our babysitter. He was very different from his older brother. He didn't like my sister at all. He would always make her go outside, and as soon as possible, he would lock the door, take off his pants, and I would lie between his legs and suck on his penis like a pacifier. I remember he would ejaculate often. Sometimes he would just fall asleep with me in his arms, and I would be filled with such a feeling of love and security.

Once, he urinated in my mouth to my complete surprise. He laughed out loud as I ran to the bathroom to spit the warm, bitter-tasting liquid out. I cried, and he picked me up and hugged me and let me lie on his belly until I stopped crying and fell asleep.

I don't know how long it went on. I think I blacked out most of those memories, but I can still see him in my mind, and I still feel an unnatural connection to him. I don't know what happened to those boys, but I have a feeling I wasn't the last child they molested.

After the first time he molested me, I started having a recurring dream. I was always being chased by something or someone trying to kill me.

Often I would fly over the mountain tops and escape from all sorts of scary-looking creatures. But sometimes, I couldn't fly high enough, and the scary beast would grab my legs and drag me down from the sky. I have had that same dream of running all my life.

CHAPTER 5

TREASURE ISLAND

After about nine months, while I was still in the third or fourth grade, we moved to a place called Treasure Island. Treasure Island is a picturesque Navy installation that lies dead center in the middle of the beautiful San Francisco Bay. The island itself is only a few miles wide and completely flat. It's a man-made island built for the 1939 Golden Gate International Exhibition. It is connected by an isthmus to a natural island called Yerba Island. It was a wonderful place to be a kid. I could see the San Francisco skyline right out my window.

I loved living on Treasure Island, and it was definitely one of the happiest times of my life. I never saw the babysitter again, but I wanted to feel more of what I felt when I was with him. I now had this belief that older chubby men meant love and affection. Following this new programming, I often made friends with other boys merely to be near their fathers.

I quickly made friends with a white boy next door. His dad was a thick, burly, bearish man, and I was drawn to him by my ever-growing sexual desire. I found him very attractive. I remember wanting to touch his furry chest with my little hands. Hairy chest instantly became another trait of my "type" that I searched for later in life. I often fantasize about him. I imagined him being my dad and sleeping in bed cuddled next to him. This clearly came from afternoons on the couch cuddling with my babysitter. I wanted to feel the same again.

The boy next door father was also my karate teacher. In fact, we were both students in his dad's karate classes. The classes took place three days a week in a town called San Bruno. My sister also took karate lessons at that time, but she didn't like it, so she stopped going. On the other hand, I continued studying and practicing martial arts for another 25 years. Years later, those lessons would end up saving my life more than once.

I remember imaging the two of us as boyfriend and girlfriend. Me being the girlfriend which just seemed natural to me. I can't remember how it happened or how often we played around. We stopped being friends after his father almost caught us naked together one afternoon in his bedroom. We were rubbing up against one another when we heard his father come home for lunch. We both panicked, and I ran and hid in the closet. I had never been so frightened in my life. I don't remember how long I waited in the closet until his dad left, but it felt like forever.

That was the first time I realized that two boys together were seen as "bad" and could get me into trouble. I was filled with terrifying fear at the prospect of getting caught and beaten by my father for doing something bad. My father had a hair-trigger temper, and I was afraid of being beaten with his leather belt.

There was a girl on our block the daughter of another neighbor. I didn't know her well, but I think she was my sister's age. She had three brothers who often had sex with her either in the bathroom or in the closet while their parents were downstairs watching TV or making dinner. I remember there was always a strange odor coming from her bedroom.

They would always get rid of me because the brothers didn't like me always trying to touch them while they were having sex with their younger sister. Eventually, they booted me out of the house, and I headed to the playground.

I was a timid kid in my early years. My poor sister was continually beating up bullies that picked on me, and boy could she fight. I don't think she ever lost a fight, at least not with a boy. When I was in the third grade, for whatever reason, two or three of the white kids playing at the playground started picking on me when my sister wasn't around. Eventually, the name-calling graduated to pushing and punching me. Naturally, I didn't stand there and let them beat me to a pulp. I knew my dad was home, and I knew he would stand up for me, so I started running as fast as I could. I made it to the house and ran inside, tears streaming down both sides of my face.

My dad asked me what happened and why I was crying. And for the moment, I felt safe, so I stopped crying and told him what happened. I was expecting him to comfort me and go yell at those mean boys. Unfortunately, that's not what my dad had in mind. What he *did* have in mind shocked the hell out of me. He grabbed me by the arm, took off his belt quite skillfully, and started whipping the crap out of me. "I ain't paying for no karate lessons for nothing, son. Stop acting like a little punk!" he shouted at me.

I was in shock and trying my best to stop crying. I was terrified to move at first. My dad told me again to stop crying, grabbed me, took me back out to the sandbox, and made me point out the kid that hit me. He then told me in front of everyone to go over and fight the boy, and if I lost, he would whip my butt some more.

I learned early on how to choose the lesser of two evils. I decided to take my chances with the boy rather than face my dad again. Without hesitation, I ran and attacked the boy with all my fury. I fought as I'd never fought before. I beat the boy up pretty badly while my father stood there and watched. That "special" experience showed me the value of fearlessness in the face of imminent danger. It also eventually made me a bully in my later years. Not for any other reason than I was more afraid of my father than fighting that boy.

CHAPTER 6

AN ALTERNATIVE EDUCATION

One day my father took me to the pool to teach me to swim. I was so excited; we stood at the edge of the pool while my father was explaining to me what to do. Then the egg hit the fan when, suddenly and without warning, he pushed me into the water.

I freaked out like nobody's business. The next thing I knew, I was flailing my arms and legs, desperate to keep my head from going underwater. Water by the gallons was pouring into my mouth. I couldn't feel the bottom of the pool, and I started to sink. And at that moment, when I thought I was dying, I looked up. My father was standing there on dry land, laughing at me like he was watching *Good Times*. That's when I really panicked. I began thinking that he was trying to kill me. I started crying, but he just stood there, smiling and looking right at me.

I don't know how, but somehow, I got my footing and eventually made it to the edge of the pool. My father reached down and pulled me out of the water and said, "Great job, son, I knew you could do it." And that's how I learned to swim.

Not too long after my aquatic debut, I was taken out of public school and sent to the gifted school, based on an IQ test with a score of 156. According to my mother, the principal at the public school suggested skipping me a grade or two. But my mother didn't want me in classes with older kids. So, instead, my teachers suggested sending me to a special school for gifted children in San Francisco.

This was no ordinary school. It was like one of those great sci-fi flicks where all the students have psychic powers, and the government wants to make them into super-soldiers or something like that. I loved it there; I learned to speak Tagalog and Spanish. The classes were unscripted and so much fun. I never had homework and was rarely asked to read any books.

I had fun at this school. My unique experience expanded my total view of reality. Among the many esoteric and intellectual lessons we were given, there was one exercise where we actually learned to remote view people and places we had never been to before. Remote viewing or RV is the ability to view impressions or images of a distant target, a lot like using extrasensory perception (ESP). We also learned how to read each other's thoughts.

One time I was paired up for an RV exercise with a blond white kid from my class. I didn't know his name and had never spoken to him before. After the teacher explained our task, I chose to be the receiver. When using this type of ESP, there has to be a sender and a receiver. The kid who I was paired with was instructed to visualize his room in detail and transmit the images in his mind to me. I would then focus my mind by clearing all my unwanted thoughts and mentally fall into sync with the other kid's mind. Try to imagine literally stepping into someone else's head.

Once I entered his mind, I was literally standing in the middle of his bedroom. As instructed earlier, I began to describe out loud everything I saw in detail. I got better after each exercise, and my accuracy improved exponentially. I was constantly being praised for what my instructors and teacher called my "natural gift."

I discovered my talent for drawing at around this time, after watching my father draw cartoons. My father was a pretty good artist. He could draw anything. I remember he used to draw beautiful pencil sketches of life-like cowboys and Indians on horses. It was always magical to watch the characters appear on the page.

More than anything, my dad and I were very competitive. I have spent my entire life trying to beat my dad at anything and everything. Sometimes I have actually won, but he would come from behind and win by some higher power or miracle most of the time. I hated him, but I respected him for his fearless and unbreakable will to win, which, in my opinion, is probably the most profound trait I inherited from him.

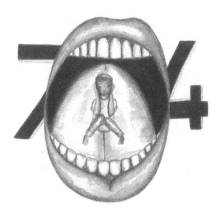

CHAPTER 7

SUMMER OF '74

The summer of 1974 rocked my happy, magical world. Things between my mother and father were changing before my eyes. Even as a little boy, I could tell they were drifting apart and were on the verge of splitting up. I figure the last straw for my mother was catching my father having sex with a white neighbor's wife in the kitchen during one of my parents' weekly parties. I know this because I walked in just as it happened. I'll never forget the hurt look on my mother's face.

After that terrible night, my mother's disdain for my father showed more and more in a mixed batch of off-handed glances and combative responses whenever my father would do or say something she didn't like. My quiet and demure mother had become more and more vocal and aggressive towards my dad overnight. They constantly fought, even to the point of physical violence. I would often hear them screaming and yelling at each other in the middle of the night.

All my father ever wanted to do was to party and be cool. Being in the Navy gave him an unbelievable amount of freedom. To this day, I have no idea what he did in the Navy. All I ever saw him do was play basketball. It was my father's out-of-control carefree attitude that would eventually teach him the lesson of a lifetime, and unfortunately, send my sister and me on a collision course straight into the depths of hell for the next five years.

Mom started to carry out her plan to convince my father to send my sister and me to stay in Texas for the summer with our grandmother. As I remember, we had only been back to Texas a couple of times before. My father finally agreed to send us off to Lubbock "for the summer."

It was 1974, and I was nine years old, my sister was 10. I cannot remember saying goodbye to my mom and dad or boarding the plane, but I remember being on it with my sister. I was thrilled. We were flying through the air just like the superheroes I was continually reading about.

When we first arrived in Lubbock, it seemed things couldn't be better. We were among a family that loved us automatically and were away from the constant partying and fighting that was going on at our house. My grandmother lived at the end of East Street, a small street with very little traffic. There were maybe ten houses on East Street in those days. My relatives lived in four or maybe five of those houses, and the rest of my relatives lived within a one-mile radius. We were a very close family back then. We often went from one relative's house to another's several times a day, drinking sodas and eating BBQ, hot dogs, and ice cream.

We often played in the middle of the street, at least until my grandmother would yell at us to get out of there before one of us got run over. Us, kids, however, were never worried about being hit by a car. Most folks drove at a snail's pace down that narrow street. They would coast down the street like a never-ending parade, and just like at a parade, people would shout out hellos and howdy to all the folks hanging out on their front porches and vice versa. There were always children playing in the yard or eating watermelon and drinking sodas. The adults often drank whiskey out of Styrofoam cups with ice and sometimes mixed it with Kool-Aid.

I believe my parents sent my sister and me away to protect us from their personal drama, but we just found ourselves in the middle of other people's drama. We were left in the care of individuals like my alcoholic grandfather, whom I don't believe I ever once saw sober. Or my pistol-packing aunts, who had the tempers of a pack of wolverines and the mouths of sailors. Not all of my aunts were mean to us, but the few who were left a mark on me that I've never forgotten.

We were kids, but that didn't seem to matter to anyone. We were treated like adults. To them, everything was normal, but for my sister and me, well, we might as well have been on Mars. Everything was foreign to us, from the food they ate, things like pigs' feet, collard greens, and neckbones, to the way they spoke and dressed. My sister and I grew up around white people in white neighborhoods. But in Texas, I was constantly picked on and even attacked by other children for "trying to sound white."

We were outsiders, and nearly everyone resented us. Again and again they asked, "Y'all think you better than us?" The truth of the matter was we never thought we were better than anyone else. We were just kids. Unfortunately, the ensuing identity crisis I developed due to "trying to be white" would also follow me for many years.

Nevertheless, I was still having fun... well, actually, too much fun playing with my cousins.

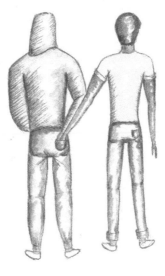

CHAPTER 8

FUN & GAMES

I can't remember how or why, but I began to play games with my cousin and two neighborhood boys, eventually leading to sexual experimentation that summer. I was surprised by how talented we were at finding excuses to get out of sight. We made up all kinds of games to play that we used as cover stories to experiment with each other's bodies.

Our favorite pretend game was the "war game." The game's objective was to hide from the enemy and try to kill everyone on the other team with our toy guns and pretend bullets. Of course, we always made sure we were on the same team.

I recall once my cousins and I decided to hide down in my auntie's storm cellar located directly across from my grandmother's front porch. I'm not sure what we were thinking or if we were thinking much at all. The three of us went down into the cellar and didn't notice my grandmother sitting on the porch watching us from afar.

There we were, down in the storm cellar, "hiding" and doing whatever we could as quickly as we could. Minutes later, we heard the cellar doors opening above us. Terror gripped the three of us, and we scrambled quickly to pull our underwear up and zip our pants. Thank God, Mary, Joseph, Moses, and Jesus Christ, my grandmother couldn't get those heavy double doors open as fast as she wanted to. She didn't see anything, but it didn't matter in the end. Our fate was sealed when she asked, "What y'all been doing down here?"

After a minute or two of silence, my grandmother noticed my cousin's zipper was down. My grandmother had eyes like a hawk. She should have been a detective because she was suspicious of everything and everyone. Nothing got past her. And when she got on a case, she would get right to the bottom of it. She began to question us. Her face had gone from morbid curiosity to enrage. The pressure was building, and I could feel my hands sweating. It was almost overwhelming, but we all kept our cool. I could see she knew something had gone on but didn't want to say it.

My grandmother decided to beat us both with a tree limb that she pulled off the tree like an executioner. And boy, let me tell you something, it hurt. She had what my dad liked to call "a field day on our behinds." After fifteen minutes of what today would be considered child abuse, my grandmother finally shouted to my cousins and me, "I better not catch neither one of y'all down in that storm cellar again, or I'm gonna beat every one of y'all's butts! Y'all hear me?"

Trust me. I haven't been back inside a storm cellar to this day. My grandmother knew how to leave an impression on a person, physically and mentally. Whether you were a child or a full-grown adult, my grandmother was someone to be feared. I don't know the truth about what happened to my grandmother as a child, but I've been told it was pretty bad for her as a little girl of mixed race. I don't know who hurt her so deeply, but what was left of her could be as cold as ice. I felt like my grandmother liked me even less after that incident. She was viciously cruel to me, and I didn't understand why. I believed that day she decided I was gay and would treat me accordingly.

One time, rumour has it that she got very upset one evening at my grandpa and chased him down East Street with a shotgun – the same shotgun she kept by her bedside. Once I found a loaded .45 Magnum in the top drawer of her nightstand.

I can never forget watching my grandmother violently beat one of my aunts with a 2x4 just because she said something my grandmother did not like. It was insane. It was literally like watching a horror film with Lizzy Borden hacking someone to death, screaming and yelling obscenities right there in front of us children.

My grandmother called me and my sister terrible names whenever she got angry. Some of her favorites were names like: "sorry," "lazy," "good for nothing," or sometimes "motherfucker" whenever she got furious enough, which was a weekly occurrence as predictable as the sunrise.

Things got so bad that I can remember being afraid of everything and everyone.. One day my grandmother decided to send us to the cotton fields to work. She said we would be paid. Of course, we had no idea what work was.

My grandmother had a sister, my great aunt that lived in Bryan, Texas. She was always so nice to me. I really liked her. Her husband was the mayor of Bryan for many years, a position he kept until he retired. All my aunts and uncles seemed to admire my great aunt. She was my grandmother's older sister, and even my grandmother was nice to her. See would get the red-carpet treatment every time she came to visit.

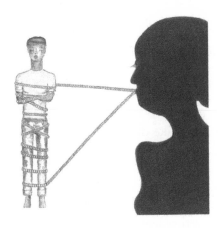

CHAPTER 9

GRANDMA DEAREST

By the end of the summer, life with my grandmother had become unbearable. She routinely abused us mentally by telling us our parents were this and that and calling my father every bad name under God's green earth. My once loving relatives told my sister and me that our father was cheating on our mother. But they didn't stop there. They also told us our mother was a bastard child. They told us our mother didn't have the same father. They said we were both born out of wedlock because of my father, making the two of us bastards as well.

Soon, more problems began with local boys picking on me and calling me a sissy. I was in constant fear of everyone around me except my sister. She protected me. She fought for me.

One day my grandmother made us go out into her backyard to work. I remember it being more like dirt with patches of grass and weeds and wildflowers surrounded by a rickety wire fence that looked like it would fall at any time. In the corner of the yard was a small oasis where she grew tomatoes. My grandmother sent us on a mission into that jungle to get all the weeds out from around her precious tomato patch. But there were a few problems. Number one, it was 109 degrees in the middle of summer in East Texas. Number two, at least 90 percent of the area was covered by thick, stubborn weeds. Number three, neither my sister nor I had ever pulled weeds before.

Saying no wasn't an option when it came to grandma dearest. So, we went out there and started pulling weeds. But at some point, my nose began to bleed violently, and I started to cry and ran in the house through the back door. When my grandmother saw me, she demanded to know what was wrong with me. I told her that my nose was bleeding, and it was too hot outside. She looked at me with hateful eyes and told me I was "sorry" and "lazy" and "good for nothing." I stopped crying and went back out into the yard and pulled those damned weeds till the sun went down with such hatred in my heart.

I felt like a slave, and I knew I'd never forgive my grandmother. I didn't like black people anymore. I started to believe black people were all unkind, cruel, and mean. During that troubled summer, my sister and I stayed as close as we could.

We did not hear from Mom and Dad much that summer. I don't remember how often they called, but when they did, my grandmother always answered the phone and would tell them that everything was "just fine." When she finally did hand us the telephone to speak to our parents, she would be right there watching us like a corrections officer, daring us to say there was anything wrong. My father would later ask us why we never told him or my mom how we were being treated. We told him because we were too scared of Grandma.

Things came to a head after a hellacious fistfight between my sister and one of our much older aunts. I can't remember if my grandmother was there when the fight happened, and I don't remember what the fight was about; all I remember is that it was terrifying. My aunt just jumped out of her chair in my grandmother's living room and attacked my sister, trying to hit her and pull her hair. I remember running across the tiny room and jumping on my aunt's back. I hit her several times in the head until she let go of my sister.

After I got her off my sister, we both ran out of the house, screaming like banshees, into the street. In the middle of the street, holding each other's hands, we screamed how much we hated being in Texas. That day we swore to each other we would never go back there again.

When my grandmother realized what was happening, she became enraged and came running out of the house after us. But we were already halfway up the street before she could catch us, thank God! We ran as fast as we could to the house of one of our aunties we could trust. We told her what had happened and that we weren't going back to Grandma's house for sure.

Not long afterward, we called my father. I remember my sister and me sobbing as we told him what my grandmother had done to us, along with all the beatings and all the cruel things that had been said to us. The next day my father was on his way to get us. He drove from California to Texas in two days... he must have driven all night and day with barely any sleep. My dad wasn't perfect, but he did love his children and was very protective of us growing up.

When he pulled up to my aunt's house, everyone could see he was not a happy camper. All of our things were still over at my grandmother's house, so we had to go over there even though we didn't want to set foot in there ever again. As soon as we walked through the door, all hell broke loose as my father and grandmother started to exchange nasty words. It was time to get out of dodge, so we left that place, and I stayed away for nearly twenty years before I returned to Lubbock again.

CHAPTER 10

HOW I LEFT YOUR FATHER

After escaping the hellfire and brimstone that was that terrible summer in Lubbock, we gratefully returned to our beloved Treasure Island, where things between my mom and dad had gone from bad to even worse.

Once my father hit my mom right in front of me. I was in shock. I tried to defend her, but my dad just picked me up and threw me out of the way. I remember hearing my mother scream. That's when I decided deep in my heart that I hated my father, and I didn't want to be anything like him.

As 1974 was coming to a close, my dad was scheduled for another nine-month sea duty on the USS Enterprise. When the day came for my father to ship out to sea, the sun was shining bright. White and grey seagulls hovered above the ship, swooping and diving from every direction. The smell of the ocean air was refreshing. The sky was beautiful as we stood there on the ship dock waving our arms, smiling, and saying goodbye.

I don't know if you've had the experience of seeing a nuclear air carrier close up, but it is a sight to behold. The ship was like a floating city with everything a kid like me loved. The Enterprise provided its crew with a game room, a basketball court, a chow hall with burgers and fries and pizza and ice cream of all flavors, jet fighter planes, and best of all, it was full of men, lots of burly, handsome, hearty sailors as far as the eye could see. All the pomp and awesome display of American Navy power took my breath away.

The ship's deck was covered with sailors of every shape and size. Black, White, Asian, and Hispanic men dressed in military whites stood side by side along the main deck, each one waving back at their families, friends, and loved ones. Crowds of people were waving American flags, homemade signs, and posters that read things like "We love you, Daddy" or "GO NAVY!"

I searched for my father among all those sailors, and, at some point, I thought I spotted him waving back at me. I don't know if I saw him, but I like to think that I did, although, at the time, I was glad he was leaving.

We stood there, my mom and my sister, watching as the ship slowly backed out of the boat dock. Little did I know my mom had made up her mind to do something none of us could have imagined.

After my father's ship sailed off into the sunset, my mother packed up everything we owned, and we drove across the country to New York City. It took six days to reach the east coast. I remember the big city lights all across the skyline as we approached New York City. The city was alluring and held me hypnotized as we drove across the famous Brooklyn Bridge that cold winter night.

New York was a very different place in the 1970s than it is today. It was a terrifying place to live in for a Navy brat from California. I can recall taking a walk down 42nd Street one afternoon with my mother. I had never seen XXX theatres, beggars, drug addicts, or prostitutes. One prostitute even tried to proposition me while standing on the corner with my mother. I was 10 years old. My mother seemed not to notice the circling street ramble, but I was frightened out of my wits and oddly fascinated at the same time.

On another corner, we came upon what, at first, I thought, was a man sleeping. As we got closer, it became clear by the smell that the man was dead. People were walking past the dead homeless man like it was normal. The city was dangerous, and we learned that lesson very quickly upon arrival.

We spent a night or two sleeping in the car. Eventually, my mother took us to the welfare office. To secure us a place to live, she told the social worker my father had died. The social worker found us short-term lodging in the attic of this extraordinary Jamaican family. I was not too fond of it. The place had a horrible smell from the old Jamaican lady cooking the same red pasta every single night. My sister and I thought she was some voodoo witch and hid whenever she came around.

I'm not sure if Mom had already secured a job with Bloomingdale's or if she got it once we reached New York. Soon, we were able to move from the Jamaicans' attic first to a project apartment in Ossining and then to White Plains, which is about an hour from downtown NYC where my mother worked. The area looked just like a scene from *The Wire*, and it had the people to match.

I remember coming out of the elevator once to a fight that had broken out in our building's downstairs lobby. A miserable older teenage boy had gotten into an argument with a teenage black girl who lived in our building. The aggressive girl violently attacked the boy, punching and kicking him like a professional fighter. At some point, the boy struck back to defend himself. I watched in horror as the girl's sisters came rushing down a nearby hallway and joined in the fight. One of the girls pulled a knife out of her purse and began to stab the boy directly in the neck and chest area.

The crowd of bystanders that had gathered screamed and shouted, egging on the fight for more violence. They seemed to find pleasure in watching the three sisters brutally assault the wounded boy. Finally, the three girls picked up the bleeding boy and pushed him through the glass door of the lobby, shattering glass everywhere.

This type of violence was nearly a daily activity in White Plains. Some poor soul was always being attacked, picked on, robbed, stabbed, raped, or molested. And soon I became one of those poor souls. On my first day of school, I was viciously attacked after class by a gang of girls because the gang leader liked me, and I had said I didn't like her.

At that point in my life, I had never seen so many black people in one place. And quite honestly, I was scared to death of going outside. I was being attacked every day, either at school or in the play yard. There was a gang of boys who hated me because – according to them – I thought I was white. They didn't like how I talked, "trying to be all proper and shit!" That same group of boys would be waiting for me nearly every day after school. I had to run home more times than I can remember to keep from being punched and kicked. The one word they used to call me that I hated the most was "faggot." Being called a "faggot" was the only thing worse than being called a "nigger."

My sister was nearly stabbed during a fight while trying to protect me from one of the local bullies. My mother, God bless her, had no clue of the horrors we were facing daily. At that point, I had developed an attitude of secrecy. I never told her about most of the violence and humiliation I suffered while living in White Plains. Without knowing the consequences, she would make us go outside to get us out of the house for whatever reason. I believe she did what she knew to do to protect and provide for her children. The only role model she had was her cruel and abusive mother. But despite it all, she was a good mother and a great provider.

When I wasn't running for my life at school, I was always finding myself in some sexual situation. I played with numerous boys—innocent touching to full contact sexual situations of various kinds. It's a shame, really, that I never knew what a normal childhood was like. In the meantime, I had forgotten all about my father. To be honest, I hoped he stayed away for good. He had hurt my mother, which made me hate him at that time. Besides, my mother gave us the impression that our father had abandoned us.

It wasn't long before my mother started bringing around her new male friend. I liked the guy, for the most part. He was a grey-haired older Jewish guy. He was a stockier fellow, which I found much more attractive than my lean build father. I remember dreaming about being his son and having a white father like in *The Brady Bunch* and *My Three Sons*. I also remember going to his house. It was much bigger and more beautiful than where we lived. I dreamed about what it would be like to be married to him. I thought of having sex with him. My youthful mind had been supplanted by my chubby male babysitter and replaced with an urge for affection driven by lust. I couldn't help myself. I wanted to regain the feeling of being safe in his arms again.

CHAPTER 11

BOYS IN MY HOOD

Little did we know that my mother was on the fast track at Bloomingdale's. She was hand-picked by one of the big-time Jewish bosses, who made her a junior executive buyer. She worked long hours, kept food on the table, and later raised our household standard of living to six figures. She did all this as a single black female without a high school diploma.

My mother's success did not come without sacrifice. We had to give up spending a lot of time together as a family. Mom was always doing what she had to do to provide her family with a better standard of life than the one she had known. As a result, she wasn't around most of the time.

I honestly can't remember my mom ever sitting down with me to do homework or to talk to me about important things about life other than the Bible. The Bible was her favorite subject, and she knew it like the back of her hand. Even as a little kid, I could quote whole chapters of the Bible I had memorized. We went to church every Sunday without fail. We went to church in the middle of snowstorms and hurricanes so that we could pray them away. Going to church every Sunday as a family was the glue that kept us all together. It was the one constant in my life.

My sister and I had to learn how to take care of ourselves at a very young age, and we learned about life by watching TV. Primetime shows like *Sanford & Son* and *Good Times* created a national perception of black people in the 70s that wasn't very flattering. The majority of the mainstream media portrayed black men as dangerous criminals, pimps, hustlers, and black women as overweight and underpaid maids and nannies.

Everything around me was telling me there was something wrong with me. I didn't like myself. The people I saw on TV, people with money, driving big fancy cars, the models, the doctors, lawyers, politicians were all white. The only thing I knew about being black was that it wasn't good. So, I wanted to be white. I loved my family, but I still wanted to be white. White men were much better looking in my mind. I rarely looked at men from other races.

As far as I knew, from watching television, all white kids had everything they wanted. They were good looking and had happy smiling faces. It was like being happy and being white went hand in hand. My family models were shows like *The Brady Bunch*, *The Partridge Family*, and *My Three Sons*. As I watched these TV programs, like most children, I believed they were somehow real.

I accepted the programming that came streaming into our home every night as the absolute standard for happy family life, and I realized we were not like those families. Therefore, something had to be wrong with me, and even worse, something had to be wrong with my family. I never told anyone growing up how I felt. It was an awful way to be so young and to have so many secrets bottled up inside.

It was around this period that I first began to wonder about who I was. Where did I come from? Why were black people being treated so differently from white people? I'd often asked myself questions like, Has it always been this way? Why did God make it like this? Why did He make me black, instead of white with blond hair and blue eyes? Why was He punishing me? Has my family or me done something wrong? Those questions planted seeds in my mind that would eventually require answers.

As a child so young and naive, I didn't know I was gay. I only knew I was physically attracted to older white husbands like the ones I saw every day on TV. I felt trapped, and I was in a constant state of confusion. As my sexual experiences grew, my attraction to older white boys/men became even stronger. I was far too afraid to tell anyone my secret, so I stayed trapped in my head. Because of my secret nature, I felt alone all the time. The only time I didn't feel alone was when a boy or man touched me in a certain way. Only then could I escape to the feelings of safety I had got from my babysitter.

I was not too fond of school, and I wouldn't say I liked New York, and worst of all, I was starting to hate myself. Fear was my constant companion and my tormentor. I went from being a happy, well-adjusted boy genius to a confused, frightened boy who didn't know who to trust. I longed for a sense of safety and security.

In 1976 my mother's career took off like a rocket. She started climbing the corporate ladder at a dizzying pace, and she took my sister and me along for the ride. We went to wonderful dinner parties and met interesting people who were either already famous or soon to be famous. We even had lunch on several occasions at the Tavern on The Green in Central Park. Seeing how the other half lived compared to us was like watching the sunrise for the first time. I also came to recognize the difference between the middle class and the people with "real money."

Meanwhile, things at school had become life-threatening for me. I was getting beat up several times a day in the boys' bathroom at school. I was assaulted and chased home every day. I could not go out into the playground during recess without being attacked. My mother had to pull me out of public school, and I enrolled in Saint Mary's Catholic School.

It was an utterly new experience for me. I remember thinking it was wonderful that we all had to wear the same uniform to school. It made everybody feel equal, which I thought was a great idea. However, it soon turned out that there were serious problems with my pious Catholic education. The teachers at St Mary's were like monsters out of a child's nightmare. The nuns were very strict, and breaking the rules was treated by physical or mental abuse or humiliation. Children were spanked regularly. The headmaster used a 3-foot wooden paddle. There was something written on it, but I don't recall what it said. There were also three rows of small holes drilled down the middle of it. Depending on the offense, a student could be given one to twenty whacks of the headmaster's paddle, and boy did those whacks hurt. Everyone cried.

I can also remember our headmistress. She was an old, nasty-tempered nun. She had to be at least sixty, but what made her look older was her permanent resting bitch face. She never looked happy, ever. I don't remember her ever smiling the entire time I was at St Mary's. This surprised me because I had grown up watching *The Flying Nun* TV series as a kid. I thought all nuns were supposed to be nice, caring, and helpful people. However, our headmistress's favorite pastime was beating my fellow students and me across the hand and knuckles with her constant companion, the dreaded 12" ruler she called 'The Hand of God.'

My sojourn at the private "holy" Catholic Church didn't last long. In 1976, my mother took us out of the school, and we also moved out of the projects. I think the final straw for her came when our apartment project caught on fire. One of the white boys we played with died that night after jumping from the 6th floor to escape the inferno.

CHAPTER 12

PRAISE THE LORD FOR CBN

It was 1978, and I was going to the seventh grade when we moved to Virginia Beach, Virginia. New York left a definite scar on my life and my sister's, but it nearly destroyed my mother.

My mother, like me, kept most things to herself. None of us knew the kind of pressure she was under while she was trying to keep up with the Joneses in the Big Apple. She had a two-hour daily commute each way into the city six days a week. And on top of all that she had to deal with the pressure of being the only black female executive at Bloomingdale's at that time.

The entire drama became too much for my mom and she was committed to Bellevue Hospital for a month after suffering a nervous breakdown. During my mom's stay at Bellevue, my dad was able to convince her to take him back and to move us all away from the terrible pressures she was facing. He also told her he was now on shore duty, which meant no more nine-month voyages away from home. We'd finally be a family again, but I don't recall being all too happy about my dad coming back, at least not at first.

So, we moved to sunny Virginia Beach, where the sky is always blue, and we started over. Virginia Beach is part of an area called the "Seven Cities," or Hampton Roads. The Hampton Roads are Suffolk, Portsmouth, Norfolk, Hampton, Newport News, Chesapeake, and Virginia Beach. Norfolk is Virginia Beach, and it is also the home of the world's largest naval station. This also made it the number one target for Russian nuclear missile strikes, but, bombs or no bombs, Virginia Beach was our new home.

It was a lovely seaside city on the Atlantic coast with miles and miles of sandy beaches, golf courses, surfing, skating, wildlife, natural parks, waterways, great food, and generally friendly people. At that time, we were living in a small three-bedroom apartment, right off Laskin Road, which was only a 30-minute bike ride to the beach.

Living in Virginia Beach was like being back in California. My sense of balance returned. We were living around white people again who spoke and acted like me. People liked me once again. I wasn't being bullied and I started making friends again.

My mom and dad getting back together came with a lot of unexpected changes, and my environment began to transform very quickly, especially in terms of our family's finances. Within a year we moved into a three-bedroom ranch style country cottage house on Wolfsnare Road. We were the only black family on the street.

My mom started working as a retail sales associate for a high-end retail store at the newly-built Lynnhaven Mall, and in a very short time, she was promoted to a management position. At the same time, my dad was finally promoted to E-7 (Chief Petty Officer). I never actually understood what my dad's actual job was, nor how much he was paid, but I do know he struggled for many years to make an E-7 pay grade. But whatever he made was a lot less than my mother's salary.

Besides the major military bases, Virginia Beach is also the home of televangelist Pat Robertson, founder of the Christian Broadcast Network (CBN). I'd never heard of CBN until my mother and father began watching Pat Robertson on TV after we moved to Virginia Beach. He was an excellent orator. He knew the Bible and he knew how to deliver 'The Word' using a sense of theatre that looked great on TV. He was, if anything, entertaining to watch.

Pat Roberson's non-profit organization raked in hundreds and hundreds of millions in donations from old ladies and people like my mom and dad who believed he was some sort of prophet from God. CBN was like a cult, and the people were like plastic. I never believed they really loved me or my family even though they would say it all the time on television. "We love you, and God wants the best for you." His holiness Pat Roberson also founded the prestigious Christian college, Regent University.

Almost overnight my parents were suddenly religious fanatics. More and more, every aspect of our lives began to center around going to church and the Bible. My parents went from the decadence of the early 1970s urban lifestyle to good Christian living, sunny beaches, suburbia, shopping malls, and crusades. My parents' conversations and their group of friends changed as well, and their attitudes shifted until they were unrecognizable. But it was my mother who changed the most profoundly.

My parents began having prayer meetings at our house several nights a week. More and more strange people came to the house to talk about the Bible, salvation, and Jesus Christ. They would stay for hours praying, crying, wailing, and speaking in strange tongues. Something was happening to my parents.

Although we lived on the white side of the city, my mother and father joined a black church over on black side of town. The church was called Mount Olive Baptist Church. And my God, let me tell you, I absolutely hated going to church. Black churches are a whole other animal than white churches. You start by getting up at 6:30 in the morning to get all decked out in your Sunday suit. My father would wake me up every Sunday morning by storming into my room and turning on all the lights, pulling the covers off me and saying something like: "We're leaving in 15 minutes, and you better be in the car."

Sunday mornings also started with Gospel music playing from my dad's prized Zenith TV/ record player/FM stereo player. It was nearly as big as the living room. Most Sundays he serenaded us with the Mighty Clouds of Joy, Keith Green, or his favorite Christian singer, Leon Pattillo.

Jesus had moved into our house, and there wasn't room for anyone else. One night the minister and his wife came over to anoint our apartment and remove anything of the devil. Everything was going pretty good at first. It was truly a miracle: my dad threw away his porno mags, and my mom tossed her Benson & Hedges cigarettes. But things quickly took a turn for the worse when the minister's wife began frantically pointing at my dog, Rascal, and saying that he was possessed by a demon.

Rascal was my beloved pet from the time I was in 3rd grade. I found him – or, should I say, he found me – walking home from school one day. He was a mixed breed. He was black with tan highlights around his face and paws, and long fluffy ears. He was just a puppy then, a couple of months old, either lost or abandoned. He was the cutest little puppy I'd ever seen, and my heart went out to him standing there staring at me with those big brown eyes. I started walking, and Rascal followed me all the way home from school. I remember taking him in the house and giving him some milk from the refrigerator. Later that afternoon, after my parents came home, I cried and begged them to let me keep him. I was actually surprised when my parents gave in.

But this time, all my pleading fell on deaf ears. I tried to hold on to Rascal as tight as I could, but my father and the preacher's wife eventually tore him from my arms. I fell on the floor bewildered. I couldn't believe my parents allowed my Rascal to be taken away from me. I was shaking as I held on to my sister, who was also crying uncontrollably and screaming her heart out. We watched as the saints of God took my puppy dog away and sentenced him to death at the city pound. I don't think I ever got over the pain and the feeling of loss that came with that experience.

The religious mayhem didn't end there. It continued at the speed of prayer, invading every corner of our world. Sometime after Rascal's martyrdom, I was told I was no longer allowed to hang out with any of my friends unless they were Christians and confessed Jesus Christ as their lord and savior. I took all this very seriously, despite the madness, because Mom and Dad had become more present and even loving. For the first time in a very long time, I felt safe. I wanted things to stay that way no matter what the cost.

I knew what I had to do. I had to give my life to Jesus Christ, then all my problems would magically go away.

I started to believe my parents were right. Maybe Jesus had come to save us. After all, we all need a savior, and I needed something or someone to believe in. As far as I was concerned, Mom and Dad were finally back together, and the lying and cheating had stopped. My dad was home, and we were a family. Praise the Lord.

I was in 7th grade when I first heard the call of Jesus Christ at Mount Olive Baptist Church. The pastor was a four-hundred-pound, fiery black preacher with thick glasses and at least four chins. He was so fat I remember wondering how he and his wife could possibly have sex together. However, he did have a gift for words and entertainment.

One Sunday during the church service, something came over me and I felt the pastor was preaching to me and me alone. I felt a stirring, something pulling from the inside, a voice calling me. I knew in that moment that I needed to be saved.

As the sermon came to a close, the preacher made the altar call asking as he had done every Sunday before, "Is there anyone here who wants to know the Savior?" I stood up and walked down the aisle and accepted Jesus Christ into my heart as my lord and savior. I remember watching my mother and father weeping tears of joy as I recited the words of faith with the pastor. I don't think I can recall ever seeing my parents happier.

When Monday morning came, I was a new-born Christian, and I dove head-first into the church and the Bible. It seemed like for the first time in my life I had found some answers. I remember standing at the bus stop waiting to go to school as I had always done, but this time I was preaching to my friends the need for salvation.

I had two best friends at the time, Ben and Jerry. Ben was a year or two older, and Jerry was my age. Ben was a big white boy who lived in the same apartment complex a few streets over. He had a massive crush on my sister as most boys did at that time. In the meantime, I had a lustful crush on Jerry. He was a chubby white boy with blond hair and a big bulge in his jeans that I tried desperately not to notice.

I told Ben and Jerry that I had found Jesus and if they wanted to keep being my friends, they must accept Lord Jesus Christ as their personal lord and savior or burn in hell forever. To my surprise, they both came over and prayed with my dad and got saved. I'm still not sure why. But they did, and so we kept doing what we always did when we weren't in church or at school.

Ben and Jerry, along with another older chubby Italian boy, and I often went into the woods that lined the neighborhood we lived in to play

"Army." The Italian boy, who was a few years older than us, was a big chubby kid with curly black hair. I secretly had a crush on him, too. Sometimes we would go to the pond where he introduced us to skinny dipping. He liked playing with himself in front of us and often ejaculated.

I often invited my newly saved friends for a sleep-over in our attic. The attic had been converted into a playroom. There was a small table where we liked to play board games, a few chairs, and two mattresses, and it turned out to be an excellent place for us to experiment. I'm not sure how the hanky-panky started, that part seems to be a blur. Nevertheless, being alone in the dark attic inspired many opportunities for boys to be boys while our parents prayed and discussed the holy Bible over tea and cupcakes below us, never suspecting a thing.

CHAPTER 13

I'VE GOT A CRUSH ON YOU!

I attended Lynnhaven Junior High where I had my first and only straight crush on a girl. Her name was Lydia. She had blonde hair, blue eyes, and high-brow features. She was like a living, breathing Barbie doll, perfect in every way. Lydia lived in a much nicer neighborhood in a big, two-story house. Her family was rich compared to mine. In fact, it became apparent very quickly that most of the other kids at Lynnhaven Junior High came from well-off families.

I'm not sure how or where my crush on Lydia came from, but it was clear to me that I was living a double life. Elementary school is very gender neutral, at least it was back then. It was okay to be a tomboy or shy or despise the opposite sex. But in junior high you were expected to date and have a girlfriend, or you were a loser. Couples paired off and formed power groups. The prettiest girls dated the most handsome guys. The best-looking couples were the top of the ladder in terms of personal power over the students and faculty.

At some point I discovered Lydia was dating the captain of the football team. His name was Harry, and he was perfect. He had white blond hair, deep blue eyes and perfectly tanned skin. He was 6ft tall with a stocky muscular build, and in the locker, he wasn't like the other boys, he was all man. Sometimes I wished I was a girl as I imagined me and Harry dating. But Harry had one flaw for all his good looks; he was dumb as a rock. I used to help him with the math homework. It's funny that some of the sexiest men I've met have also been some of the dumbest.

While other boys dreamed of hot models, marriage, children, expensive cars, and corporate jobs, I dreamed of marrying older daddy bears. Guys like Steve Austin on the TV series *The Six Million Dollar Man* were very attractive to me in those days.

Just before my second year of junior high, my family moved again, and in doing so we upgraded again. This time my parents rented a house in a much nicer neighborhood called Windsor Woods. Windsor Woods was the epitome of Virginia Beach's middle and upper middle-class suburbs in 1979 and was in the "right" part of town. As I look back on that time,

I have a better understanding of the financial and physical commitment my mother and father made in order to provide me and my sister with a better life.

Great Neck Road was – and still is – one of the wealthiest and nicest areas in Virginia Beach to live. The further you went down Great Neck Road, the bigger and more beautiful the houses became until you reached the inlet. Back then the homes in the area were spectacular, million-dollar beach homes which sat along the water. We lived at the beginning of Great Neck Road. My family was one of only two black families living in Windsor Woods. In fact, as I recall, including us, there were only three black families in the entire Great Neck area.

We did, however, have a small collection of black kids at Cox High School. They were bussed over from the low-income neighborhood called Seatack. These unprivileged kids lived in Virginia Beach's absolute worst area off Birdneck Road. It was a collection of shacks, trailer park homes, and small government-assisted housing apartments.

The strange thing about the black kids from Seatack was that although they came from poverty, they always dressed up for school. They wore designer jeans and expensive glasses and two-hundred-dollar basketball shoes. It was like they wanted everyone to believe they had money, but everybody already knew these kids were poor. And compared to the rich white kids that went to Cox High School, they were dirt poor.

Honestly, all they actually did with that behavior was make the white kids laugh behind their backs. I can remember on many occasions listening to my white friends talk about how stupid those black kids from Seatack were for spending their money on clothes and cars while living in shacks. The rich white kids who lived in ten-thousand-square-foot homes on the water were the exact opposite when it came to money and being flashy. They wore Van Halen, AC/DC, and Rolling Stones T-shirts, holey jeans, flip flops, and Vans and drove trucks and Japanese cars.

The only reason I knew I was different from the other black kids was because whenever my white friends slipped and started making racist jokes or comments, they would catch themselves and say, "I don't mean you" or "I'm talking about them," and "I don't think of you as black... You're not like them." Talk about a mindfuck.

The turn of the decade ushered in a new wave of teenage rebellion. It was a ticking time bomb that exploded on shows like *Saturday Night Live* and MTV. The world had gone from disco to punk rock, hair bands, and a new genre called hip hop. Overall life in America was better than it had ever been before. I was still being picked on, but not as much, and most of all, I was fighting back. I began to build a reputation as a fighter.

My sister really blossomed in junior high. She was so pretty and so confident. She was a pom pom girl, a member of the field hockey team, and a star sprinter on the girls' track team. In fact, my sister was so popular that I was given a pass from a lot of people who typically would not have given me the time of day in junior high just by default. It was like just being my sister's brother made me instantly cool and liked by complete strangers.

School was always easy for me. I never studied and rarely did my homework. I was an "A,B,C,D" student. I don't think my mom and dad paid much attention to my grades as long as I didn't fail anything – no one really said much about it.

CHAPTER 14

A SERIES OF UNFORTUNATE EVENTS

My father started taking me along with him to work out my last year of junior high. His favorite gym was on Oceana Navy Base, mainly because they had great ping-pong tables and great players. I had a plan to try out for football and basketball in high school, so the idea was to spend the summer training in the gym while my dad worked out or played ping-pong.

The first time I watched my dad play ping-pong, I instantly fell in love with the game. I was hooked. My dad and the other players were amazing. It is not a well-known fact, but table tennis is one of the most popular individual sports in the world. There were all sorts of players: Egyptians,

Nigerians, Chinese, and Europeans, and some guys even played on their home country's national teams before coming to America. They could hit the ball from inches off the ground and send the ball spinning back to the underside of the table and incredible speeds. I watched players smash a high ball with all their might only to have their opponent return it from 20 feet off the table.

I was blown away. I had discovered a sport that I really loved. My dad had expected me to play manly sports like basketball or track or football; after all, I was my dad's son, and my dad was a manly man and a sports junkie. He played golf, squash, handball, he swam, and he liked to fish. But table tennis was his favorite sport.

So, I started going to the gym every day to play table tennis. I trained with coaches and fellow table tennis players. I usually divided my training time into 80 percent table tennis and twenty percent martial arts. After all I was dedicated to being the best table tennis player in the world.

One day, while at the gym, I made a surprising discovery. I was waiting for my turn to play and decided to go into the weight room and work out while I waited. After a few minutes, nature called and I headed to the men's bathroom, but the one I usually went to was closed for cleaning. I knew there was another bathroom, but hardly anyone used it because it was on the other side of the gym. However, I had to set out to find it.

I got to the other side of the gym, went into the first stall and sat down. I looked to the left of me and noticed a grapefruit-sized round hole that looked like it had been cut out with a screwdriver. I could see a man sitting there in his Navy uniform and white sailors cap. I could see his face, his nicely trimmed beard, and his blue eyes staring right at me. His Navy issue blue dungarees were down around his shiny, patent leather shoes. I also saw what he had in his hand, and as I looked up at him, I saw the way he was looking at me.

Suddenly, I was so confused. It was just like when I was a little boy. I kept looking through the hole. He started masturbating without saying anything. I didn't move. I just kept looking as he gestured for me to come closer. I started to reach my twelve-year-old hand through the hole, but, all of a sudden, I could hear my father calling me. I freaked. My little butt jumped up from the toilet seat before my mind could finish the thought. I got out of that bathroom stall as fast as I could and hustled over to the sink, pretending to wash my hands as my father came storming through the door demanding to know where I had been.

I felt like a mouse caught in a trap. I was shaking with fear, and my chest was about to explode into a thousand pieces. But on the inside, I was intoxicated by a deadly mixture of fear and excitement. I didn't want to leave; I kept looking back as I quickly walked back to the other side of the gym. Eventually, I would go back, again, and again, and again. In fact, the gym became my second home.

Over time, I discovered other areas of the gym and the surrounding buildings where men could be found. I wasn't aware of the labels of gay, bi and straight at that age; they were just men to me. I faithfully continued meeting strange men in bathroom stalls, saunas, showers and in other areas of the men's locker room from 8th grade all the way until my senior year.

I played table tennis, practiced kung fu, or worked out eighty percent of my time every day all the way through my junior high and high school years. I probably spent the rest of my time being molested by white Navy officers and enlisted men. Years later, when I came out to my parents, I remember my father saying to me, "I wondered why you spent so much time in the sauna. I thought you were trying to make weight for the wrestling team."

My poor father, he really wanted to believe I was training the entire time. But the fact was that for five years, just yards away from him, his son was being molested by complete strangers day after day. I don't know if he ever suspected or if he was just too busy playing table tennis or basketball. I can't remember how many men molested me. I never even knew their names. Some of them I never saw again, while some became regulars, especially the lunchtime bathroom stall molesters.

Sometimes when I was playing a ping pong game against someone, I'd let them win so I could hurry and get back to the sauna if I saw a man I recognized going that direction. There was an unspoken body language I learned to recognize from the men that molested me. There was a particular type of eye contact that gave them away. These men would look right into my eyes, and then linger for just a moment too long. Straight men don't make intense lingering eye contact with other men unless they are fighting or competing with one another.

I guess you could say I lost my virginity in the saunas on the Little Creek Navy Base. The man who took my virginity was an older white Navy officer. He was in his late twenties or early thirties with brown hair and brown eyes. He seemed a bit creepy at first. When I first walked in the sauna, he kept staring at me with this depraved look on his face. He told me his name was Tom. He was a goofy-looking fellow who would pass for a nerd by today's standards. He had to be a real pervert to want to sodomize a 12-year-old boy in a public sauna.

About a week later, I was in the sauna with that same nerdish man. There were a lot of people at the gym at the time and we almost got caught. We both walked out of the sauna, and I followed him to the showers. While we were pretending to shower, the man told me to follow him to his car. I was so scared, but I followed him anyway. In the parking lot, we both got into his car, and we drove around for a few minutes until he found a private-looking place to park. After parking, he reached down and started undoing his pants. He told me that he wanted me to give him a blow job, and in return he was going to give me a "vanilla milkshake."

After a few minutes, I could hear the man moaning. He was hurting me, forcing my head down. Then I heard him say out loud, "Here's your milkshake." Involuntarily, I vomited all over the front seat of his car.

Deep inside I started to not like myself for what I was doing and what I was letting these men do to me. I was so confused. This wasn't the love I dreamed of as a boy. No holding hands, kissing or affection of any kind. It was purely sexual gratification for an endless parade of perfect strangers. I knew in my heart what I was doing was wrong. But I couldn't stop myself. Sex became an addiction.

I wanted to be loved, like all my friends at school who clearly got lots of love from their girlfriends and boyfriends all the time. Although sex was always being discussed, especially among the boys at my school, I didn't know what love was. I would just listen to what the other kids said, and I imagined what it was like to be in love and to walk down the hallway holding hands, lightly kiss each other on the lips, out in public for everyone to see. That was alien to me, as I sought love in the shadows and behind closed doors.

I never spoke of what happened to me in that car to anyone until now. As vulgar as the incident was, I felt nothing. I was numb emotionally. My sense of morality and innocence was taken from me by the hands of my "babysitter" another lifetime ago.

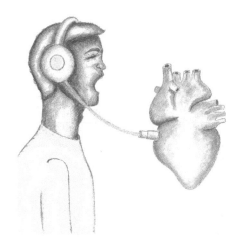

CHAPTER 15

NEVER MIND THE BOLLOCKS, IT'S HIGH SCHOOL

My personality had changed dramatically by the time I hit high school. The 1980s were the Reagan years, and the war on drugs was in full throttle. Black neighborhoods were invaded by crack, and crime was on the rise, even in the suburbs. Bands like Blondie, Queen, AC/DC, Ozzy, and Rush dominated the airwaves. Anita Bryant had made herself public enemy #1 to the gay liberation movement that was growing by the day. America was the most prosperous nation on earth. The world would never be the same.

High school was when I started to grow my "sea legs." I had developed an image as the cool black kid that everyone envied. I was cool with the punks, the jocks, the nerds, the potheads, the deadheads, the new waves, the rich kids, and the black kids. I was no longer shy. I had become the class clown, always joking and goofing off during class.

I deliberately avoided hanging around after school to hang out with kids my age mainly because 90 percent of the students at Cox High School were smoking pot and drinking before, during and after school. I wasn't into that. After watching the effects of drugs and alcohol on my father, I wanted nothing to do with people who drank or used drugs. And besides, I was a Christian.

On the outside I seemed like a normal kid, but I was far from normal. On the inside, I was living in constant fear. I was struggling to stay afloat in a sea of guilt. I was barely keeping my head above water most of the time. I felt there were multiple "Houstons" in high school. There was Houston, the little boy, Houston, the man, Houston, the athlete, Houston, the perfect son who always did what his parents asked, Houston, the Christian, Houston, the rebel, Houston, the homosexual, and Houston, the molestation victim.

It's difficult for me to describe how hard it was at that age to go through high school watching everyone I knew and didn't know dating and sharing public affection. Even the ugliest guys had girlfriends. I, however, was terrified of girls. I didn't understand them at all, nor did I want to understand them. Girls in my high school were like aliens to me. I feared they would be able to read my mind and discover I was really a "faggot" in disguise. They would definitely expose me to everyone. I was constantly reminded of a kid that I went to junior high with who committed suicide as a result of public shaming at school. I can't say for sure what I would have done if I had been discovered, but suicide was not off the table by any means. I couldn't let that happen, so I kept my distance when it came to friendships with girls.

High school was also a place where I learned to give everyone and everything labels. Labels identify a person's social value, which determines how that person should be treated within the social environment. In the 1980s, being labelled a faggot was the kiss of death, you were fair game to be bullied and ridiculed and even beaten up by everyone.

At Cox High School the "faggots" were in art class, band, and theatre. I never took these classes. Instead, I tried out for the football team, because I wanted to be in the locker room with the big white boys. I was terrible at football, and quite honestly, I was scared shitless of some of the players. These guys were huge, at least twice my size. I hated being tackled by those 300-pound elephants.

At times in the locker room, I struggled to hide my arousal. A couple of times I had to avoid the showers for fear of getting an erection. To my relief the coach cut me from the team after a few weeks of practices.

I tried out for basketball, but again I was cut. I wasn't that great, and I definitely was too short. I was 5'6" standing next to 6+ feet giants. So, next I joined the track team. Turns out anyone can join the track team. I ran cross country, the mile and the two-mile.

Next, I decided to join the wrestling team. I had wrestled my last year of junior high, where I had a huge crush on a guy named Jeff, who was in one of my classes. Jeff was a national champion and one of the smartest kids I ever met. He was listed in the *Who's Who* of students in the nation. We became friends and our friendship continued until we got to Cox.

Thanks to all the time I spent at the gym, my body had changed, and I went from the chubby, awkward kid in elementary school and junior high to a super badass with a body like Bruce Lee. I was looking good, and there was no shortage of girls that wanted to date me.

I did eventually pretend to date a girl named Elaine. She was one of the prettiest girls in school. She had a beautiful smile, perfect skin color, big bright brown eyes. She was a transfer student from New York, and she was half black and half Puerto Rican. My heart goes out to Elaine. Through no fault of her own, she fell in love with someone who was physically unable to love her the way a woman needs to be loved. My brain and my body had already been hardwired to sexually respond to chubby white men.

I can't help but wonder who I'd be if I hadn't been molested? Maybe we'd have gotten married. Maybe I'd be a father of three with a house and a pretty wife and a great job in an office somewhere. Maybe Elaine and I would have been real high school sweethearts. Perhaps, I wouldn't have pretended I was too drunk to fuck when the "big moment" happened on prom night. I can still see the disappointment on Elaine's face. It was one of the hardest things I've ever had to go through. I did care about her, and I never meant to hurt her, but I just couldn't do it. She looked heartbroken that night. We broke up a few days later.

My high school years were great, but by then I was addicted to anonymous sex with strangers. I remember one time my father told me he couldn't take me to the gym. So, rather than stay home, I rode my bike the entire 10 miles down Great Neck Road to Shore Drive, which was a two-lane road that ran along the oceanfront. I did ten miles in 30 minutes so that I would be at the gym before lunchtime when the sauna got busiest. Looking back, I can't believe I rode my bike that far on that dangerous narrow road to go "work out."

My prison was the sound of silence. I hated what I was turning into, but I didn't know how to stop it. I knew from reading the Bible that fornication was a sin, but I never once thought the fault was with the men who were molesting me. I blamed myself every time, and my guilt grew.

Fear was my constant companion; fear of my parents finding out, fear of friends finding out, and fear of being hated by my family and friends. I thought that everyone would laugh at me and hate me if they knew what I was doing with those men. The Church said homosexuals were demon-possessed sinners. The Bible said God hated homosexuals so much he wiped out all the wicked people of Sodom and Gomorrah. Whether I was going to school, coming home, going to church, every waking moment, I was utterly terrified of being found out.

I was broken and confused, and my wounds were slowly bleeding out. The problem was that by staying silent I was allowing the molestation to continue. You see, molesters are a lot like sharks: they can sense blood in the water from miles away. And these sharks followed me everywhere I went.

In 1981 my father sent me to the US Open with Jerry Life, my table tennis coach at the time. I'd already won the Junior State Championship, and I was a three-time state champion in my age group. Playing at the US Open was the next step for me towards Olympic gold.

The 1981 Table Tennis Open was held at Princeton University, New Jersey, and I was on cloud nine when I arrived. It was a dream come true, and I was having the time of my life. The event was held in a huge auditorium. On the main floor were at least 100 tables, all separated by small two-three-foot partitions that created the individual playing spaces for matches. I was wearing my brand-new table tennis shoes and my Stiga warm-up suit. Before I left, my dad bought me a brand-new paddle and rubber. It was a special carbon racket that cost $200 back then. I looked like a pro.

I felt great and I was ready; all my training was for this moment. I was playing against, meeting, and making new friends with the best players in the world. I won a few matches, but I was eventually eliminated by an incredible Swedish kid. Nevertheless, the experience was priceless, and for the first time I was on my way to the Olympics.

On the last night of the Open, my coach decided to go back to his room early due to a wrist injury he had suffered. After I finished playing, I watched the top players in the adult matches play for a while. I wasn't feeling very tired, and I didn't want to just go back to my room and sit there bored. So, I decided to walk around and see the campus. It was Princeton after all.

While I was walking across the campus, I came across an older white man between thirty and forty with a beard. I remember he was wearing a light-colored jacket, tan shorts, a white T-shirt, and sneakers. He had bushy black hair and was sitting on a bench under a row of trees up against the bushes. He was looking at me. I smiled at him and he began to rub himself. I remember standing there not knowing what to do. Then suddenly the man waved his hand and gestured for me to come over to the bench. I sat down next to him, and he asked if I'd like to go with him, pointing to a nearby building.

When we got behind the building, he quickly pulled his shorts down, grabbed me from behind and pushed me up against the wall, forcing my shorts down. He spat in his hand and forcibly penetrated me. The pain was terrible. He covered my mouth and told me to relax, it will be okay. I could hear him breathing heavily behind me, and I was really afraid. Then, about a minute later, the man gave off a quiet sigh and stopped moving. He pulled his shorts back on and zipped them up.

The man then asked me how old I was, and why I was here. I told him I was 14 and that I was here playing table tennis at the US Open. He smiled at me, said thank you, and left. I didn't understand what he was thanking me for at the time, and I didn't realize I had just been raped. I still remember the pain and the confusing feelings I was left to deal with that night. I did my best to hide my emotions and the pain for the rest of the trip. After a few days I forgot all about the rape, and I never told anyone about it until now.

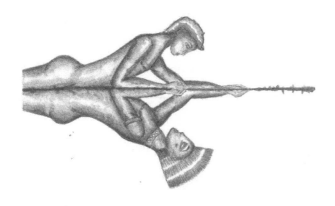

CHAPTER 16

A PUNK IS BORN

I made a bit of a name for myself by my senior year in high school. I was no longer my sister's little brother. I was Houston, the kung fu expert and Christian punk rocker. I was covering up so much inside. I was a different person altogether at school, a complete fraud, in more ways than one. I'd tell myself that I am no different from everyone else. Back then, gays were sissies. But I knew I was different because my classmates would often say things about me like, "Houston... he's a cool dude, he's a badass motherfucker." I had respect, and I did everything to keep it.

All around me, everyone I knew was sexually active. When I was in junior high, one of the black girls from Seatack had to drop out of school because an English teacher got her pregnant. Football and wrestling coaches and even the janitors were caught and prosecuted for having sex and doing cocaine with cheerleaders. One of my sister's friends from a family in our neighborhood had to flee the city under death threat because her father, a boy scout leader, got caught molesting the 12-year-old boy scouts.

A young girl was raped and left for dead in the woods near her school. The boy who did it was much older than the little girl. He tried to cover the body with leaves. Another boy we knew killed his dentist in the dentist's examination room. He told the police the dentist tried to touch him in his groin, so he beat the man to death. That boy was 16, and he was never charged with a crime. The murder of the gay dentist became the talk of the town overnight. At church, at school, at the grocery store, everyone was talking about it.

Nearly every straight guy I spoke to about the murder said the dentist deserved it. "If a fag put his hands on me, I would kill him too." I took those hate-filled words to heart. I wasn't going to let that happen to me, so I doubled down on my martial arts training. I was only a teenager, but I trained and fought grown men. I was in incredible shape. Surprising my opponent with my skill level was my specialty. Winning meant respect from other males, and it also proved my straightness to any doubters.

All that time in the gym and the years of martial arts had turned me into a bit of a badass. I'd actually grown to love fighting, and I was one hell of a fighter. By the time I turned 16, I was fighting national champions. But I stopped going to tournaments because I was constantly disqualified for excessive violence. I was ready to fight anyone, anywhere, anytime. And for the most part, I did just that. I was a real prick, but a likable prick.

I was suspended several times in high school for fighting and other violent behavior. One time I was in the principal's office for putting a No. 2 pencil through another student's hand because he tried to steal my ice cream sandwich. When we got to the office, my father was there with the other kid's father. I sat down next to my dad, and the other boy sat next to his. The principal told my dad the details of what had occurred in the lunchroom. When he was finished, he asked my father what he was going to do about it. My dad stood up, smiled, and said, "The kid should not have messed with my son."

Even though I was suspended for two weeks, my father was very proud of the fact that his son was a martial expert. The more I fought and won, the more he praised me. He would tell people, "My son is a black belt" even though I wasn't. I only got as far as a brown belt because we moved so many times I was constantly starting over with a new teacher and a new martial arts style. Winning became everything to me. The truth was I was more afraid of losing than anything, and that gave me the will to win. My dad told me every day, *"Almost* don't count, son, except in Horseshoes & Hand Grenades." I wanted to be the best.

In the midst of all this, I found myself waking up every morning, pretending to be straight and wondering why I was different. Why wasn't I like other boys? Why did God do this to me? Why would he let me have feelings for someone and then put me in a world where I'm not allowed to do or say anything about the way I felt? All those trapped feelings found their outlet in 1992, the day I met Bobby D.

Bobby D. was a skinny, pasting looking white boy with bad acne. He was a smart kid and a math wizard. He was one of a small group of kids that were calling themselves "punk rockers." They were all as weird as they come. They were labeled social outcasts and losers by the cool kids like the jocks and cheerleaders.

Bobby D. sported a peacock-like blue and pink mohawk and a pair of thick square glasses with a strap that kept them from falling off. He had pushed safety pins through both his ears and his left nostril. He wore ripped T-shirts of arcane punk bands like GBH, Black Flag, and his favorite, the Sex Pistols. He wore a pair of red Doc Martens boots with white laces, which I thought was the coolest thing I'd ever seen. And like all real punks at that time, Bobby was a skateboarder.

Bobby D and I became fast friends after I stopped a couple of football jocks from kicking Bobby's tail one day in the hallway after class. I saw the guys bullying him about an American flag he had safety-pinned upside down to the back of his T-shirt. It was two against one, and I didn't think it was a fair fight. So, I walked over and told the two jocks that if they didn't back-off, I'd jump into the fight. Everyone knew my reputation by then, so the two jocks backed down and walked away. They mumbled a few things under their breath, but that was the end of that.

I was genuinely surprised at how thankful Bobby D. was to me for helping him. It wasn't a big deal as far as I was concerned. I just didn't like watching anyone get bullied. After talking for a minute or two, Bobby invited me to his house after school to listen to some music. When we got to his house, he put on the record that changed everything. The name of the album was "Anarchy in the UK" by the Sex Pistols. It was a political and social revelation for me. I'd never heard music like it before! To say I was blown away would be an understatement.

Punk bands back then weren't polished like bands today. They were terrible musicians, but they had created a distinctive sound that was raw in your face and powerful. With overdriven, distorted guitars lacing, it was loud, driving four-on-the-floor straightforward basslines. The punk movement was a social protest through music. The lyrics were raw and politically centered, and I loved it! The thick British accents were pretty cool, too.

The Sex Pistols lead singer, Johnny Rotten, wasn't singing. He was screaming, venting his bottled-up anger and aggression at the system, and I identified with that anger. I wanted to scream too. I was confused, and I was disappointed at God for the cards I'd been dealt. From that day forward, I, too, was a punk rocker. I wanted to be free to express myself. I was already different from everyone at my school. As far as I knew, I was the only gay in my school.

That same afternoon, Bobby D. gave me my first mohawk, well, it was more like a strip of hair down the middle of my head. He used a pair of dog clippers that were out in his parents' garage. We then decided to dye my "mohawk" red. I poked a safety pin through my right ear. (Bobby D. had informed me piercing the left ear meant you were gay.)

When I got home, I walked into the living room as a newly-born punk rocker. My mother and father almost passed out. After the shock wore off, my parents got angry at me and demanded I cut my hair. My father tried to rip the safety pin out of my ear, but I blocked his hand so fast I think I frightened him. My father gained a healthy fear of my martial arts skills after I nearly broke his back during some backyard sparring.

That was the first time I said no to my parents. I was 15 and no longer afraid of my father. I remember taking the safety pin out because it did look a bit silly, but I didn't cut off my mohawk. I was proud of it. When I went to school the next day, I was a new person. I got high-fives and "Dude, your hair is rad" from nearly everyone that saw me. I was unique, and people noticed me. I had my own identity at last. I was Houston, the punk rocker!

After a few days, my mom and dad finally accepted the fact that I wasn't going to cut off my mohawk. "You know you're going to have to go to church looking like that, son!" But I didn't care, because from that moment on I was never the same person again. Punk rock music was my emancipation.

I also knew I wanted to be a singer in a punk band and write great lyrics, so I joined a band during lunch at the school cafeteria. An Asian kid I didn't know walked over to me and told me he was in a punk band called the Dead Scouts and asked me if I could sing. Although Mom made my sister and me take piano, saxophone, clarinet, drums, and trumpet lessons as a kid in California, I couldn't sing or play. However, I lied and said yes. They couldn't play a lick, but that made it punk. Instead of singing, I just screamed in cadence with the drums. It turns out I have a voice for "alternative styles of singing." Everyone said my voice sounded crazy cool amplified and with effects like chorus or delay.

We didn't stay together for more than a couple of months. The band eventually found another singer who looked cooler and sang a lot better. I found out I was no longer in the band when I showed up for practice. I walked into the practice space, and I was introduced to the new singer. I already knew who he was. His name was Deek, and he lived in my neighborhood. I can't say we were friends, but we knew each other. He was a good-looking guy with full, thick, jet-black hair and the type of blue, silvery eyes that made him look like an alien. He was thin with a chiseled, handsome face, a cocky attitude, and a body like a rock star.

After getting kicked out of my first band, Bobby and I decided to start our own band. He was the singer, and I was the bass player. Now we needed gear. We didn't have any money, so Bobby D. came up with a solution. We walked across the street and stole a Peavey T-40 bass from our church.

Punk gave me a whole new identity, and my cool points at school skyrocketed. I was on a new level overnight, and my status at school grew. Suddenly, I was an influencer. People wanted to be seen around me and be like me. Kids started listening to punk and wearing clothes like mine. In 1981 there were only a handful of punkers, and I was the only black guy in school who was a "punk rocker." For some reason, the white kids thought that was the coolest thing ever.

CHAPTER 17

LGBTQ- FEVER

The first time I went to a gay bar was in 1982. My sister had developed into a party girl, to my parents' horror. She ran with a crowd of rich white girls, who all thought their poop didn't stink. My sister and her popular friends went out almost every weekend to school parties, house parties on the beach, and bars. I didn't like going to those parties, mainly because I was afraid of being discovered if some girl wanted to make out with me.

One night right before my sister's graduation, I was downstairs in the living room watching TV and doing push-ups and sit-ups during the commercial breaks. The doorbell rang, but I didn't get up to answer it because it was never for me. As the bell wouldn't stop ringing, I went to the door and opened it, and there behind the door was my sister's best party buddy, Terri. She was too pretty for her own good. She came from a good family with a brother I never met and parents who could not control her in any shape or form.

Terri came in, all smiles and playing with her blond hair, looking like she was already feeling her alcohol. She told me that my sister and her circle were going to a place called the Boat House over in Norfolk. Normally my sister didn't invite me to go out with her and friends. I'm sure it was partly because I didn't want to go, mainly because I had stopped listening to anything other than punk rock music. Also, I didn't drink or smoke, and as far as everyone knew, I was still a virgin. So, for everyone that knew me, I was like the Adam Ant song "...goodie two shoes, don't drink, don't smoke, what do you do..."

The first thing I realized as we entered the club that night was the strange-looking black woman at the door. There was something not quite right with her, but I couldn't quite put my finger on it at the time. After we entered the club, I followed my sister and her friends straight to the dance floor. The music and lights were amazing. I'd never heard music so loud before. It was like I was teleported to another world.

We entered the dance area, stood together in a circle, and started dancing our asses off as if we owned the place. Ironically, the song that was playing was "It's Raining Men" by The Weather Girls. That's when I noticed something else odd about the bar. I didn't see any women. Except for my sister and Terri, the bar was 100% male bodies around us, dancing and rubbing up against each other to the music. At first, I tried to look away, but then my sister and her friends looked at me, and smiling, they said, "It's a gay bar." That was the first time I'd ever heard the two words put together in a sentence. Was this a sign from God? Was this the place for me? I knew I had to find out, and I knew I'd be back.

A few weeks later, my sister took off to Atlanta to go to college, and I began sneaking out of the house late at night to go to the bars. I'm not sure how or why I could get into those gay bars, considering that I was still in high school, but they always seemed to let me in.

I met many men in those bars, and they took full advantage of my naivety and youth. Each time, I thought to myself, this one will like me, this one will fall in love with me, this time we'll be together. But it never happened. The more I tried to please them, the more I allowed myself to be used.

My dream was still to play ping-pong in the Olympics before graduation. I was presented with the opportunity to go to China and train with the world's best coaches, but unfortunately, my parents couldn't afford the cost involved for me to go. My dad came up with the idea that I should join the Army rather than going straight to college. He said he'd spoken to a recruiter who told him if I joined the Army, not only would the Army pay for my training, but I could be stationed in Germany, where the best players in the world competed in the European leagues. So, being the "good son" that I was, I went to the recruiting office with my father and signed up for the Army. Actually, my father had to sign for me because I was just 16. That decision, however, would turn out to be one of the biggest mistakes of my life.

After graduation, in 1983, I decided to go to Atlanta to spend the summer with my sister, who was studying fashion design at the Art Institute of Atlanta. It was one of the most exciting times of my life. Atlanta was a big city full of exciting people. Here, I rediscovered my love of dancing and went from punk rocker to club kid. At the time, Madonna, Prince, Eurythmics, Depeche Mode, Grace Jones, were all pushing the limits of gender-bending and what was acceptable in the mainstream. Michael Jackson had just released his smash hit album "Thriller."

In those years, we had, for the first time, openly gay artists and groups like Culture Club, Bronski Beat, Sylvester, Divine, and Soft Cell. I instantly gravitated to those groups and their sense of style. I even started to wear the eyeliner and makeup my sister and her friends let me borrow. It was the eighties, and the androgynous look was very much in fashion. I even wore skirts with punk rock T-shirts and combat boots. I was the first guy in Atlanta to wear a skirt (no kilt) to the bars. Everyone loved it and copied my style.

Most of my influences came from my sister and her roommates at that time. After all, they were all models and regular dancers on a wildly popular Atlanta television show called the "Dance Show," which came on every Saturday afternoon. No one at that time knew about me or even thought that I might be gay, so my sister didn't think anything about taking me out to notorious gay bars like The Saint, Backstreet, Weekends, or the world-famous drag bar, Illusions.

CHAPTER 18

DANCING QUEENS

The early eighties were also the beginning of a cultural revolution, fueled by drugs, high energy music, and dancing, literally in that order. If you could dance, you were instantly a star. My sister and her friends were the queens of the ball. Everywhere we went, everyone knew them. They were always VIP, and my sister's face was on billboards and television. She even landed parts in two movies. She was unofficially crowned the Limelight's dancing queen, and just like back at home, she was incredibly popular, and everybody loved her.

Everything we did was centered around going out to the clubs to dance. I can't honestly remember eating much, except for a lot of peanut butter and syrup sandwiches. It wasn't like we were broke. We just spent all the money my parents sent every week on buying new clothes to go out with, and of course, new records to dance to and, apparently, a lot of cocaine.

At that time, I didn't know what cocaine was, and my sister, God bless her heart, was very cautious about keeping her friends' partying away from me. And she did an excellent job because I was utterly clueless about what was going on around me. Her friends had all been partying their asses off in those bathroom stalls, right under my nose. I remember wondering why they were always going to the bathroom.

Every morning at the apartment was the same that entire summer. We'd wake up every day in the late afternoon, and the first thing we would do was to turn on the record player and start practicing our dancing. After a few hours of dancing, we spent the next few hours figuring out what to wear that night.

We never wore the same thing twice, and always looked like stars! My sister and the other girls would literally take hours to get dressed and put on their makeup. I often stood and watched. Honestly, my sister and her roommates were all gorgeous girls, and I remember wanting to be like them. Then one day, I went down the hall to wake up one of the girls, and when she answered the door, I didn't recognize her. She literally looked like a ghost. That's when I discovered the power of makeup.

I was having the time of my life. Every night we were at a gay bar dancing the night away. Of course, I never let on that I was gay, and oddly enough, no one ever suspected that I was, even after I disappeared a couple of nights and didn't return till the next day. It was one of those nights when I "disappeared" that I first discovered what gay men called "cruising" at a trendy place in the city called Piedmont Park.

That night we were at a favorite after-hours gay bar named Backstreet. It was a big place, and it had at least three jammed-packed floors with gay men and a handful of women, or what gay men affectionately call "fag-hags." The place was jumping, the music was pulsing and loud, and the dance floor was packed shoulder to shoulder.

My sister and her friends were dancing their asses off and left me on my own. I saw men all around and felt overwhelmed. I suddenly remembered a bar next door, The Cove, that intrigued me as we were coming into Backstreet. I decided to go there.

To my surprise, they let me in immediately. The place was dark with fantastic music I'd never heard before. It was underground "gay bar" music; the beat was dark, driving, and sexual, and the bass made your teeth rattle. There were men everywhere dressed in leather jackets, blue jeans, and leather chaps with jockstraps and black leather boots. These were "leather men." Everyone was shirtless, and some wore nothing but their underwear.

Men were blowing whistles, and one or two of them were twirling colored flags as they danced.

I remember smelling a strange odor in the air; it was intense, like the smell of ammonia. The aroma was coming from a small bottle passed around that had RUSH written on it in big red letters. I joined the party and danced until the end of the night. I even tried the bottle of Rush as it wound its way around the dance floor. As I took a big sniff, my head started spinning out of control.

At the end of the night, I started to panic as I realized that Backstreet was closed, and I didn't have a ride home. I was standing out front trying to figure out what to do when an older man invited me to go with him to the park. He said it would be fun. As we walked along the trail, I started to see men all around us having sex in the woods. We stopped, and there in the park, he molested me.

After it was over, he asked how old I was, and I told him I would be eighteen in November. I told him I didn't have a way home, so he invited me back to his place. I ended up staying much longer than I wanted. I kept telling the guy that I wanted to go home, but he just ignored my request until the next day when he finally dropped me off around the corner from my sister's apartment.

My sister and the girls didn't seem that worried, but they did ask where I'd been. I told them I had met a girl and spent the night at her place and then hung out the rest of the day. That was the last time I remember "slipping" away.

Maybe my extreme confidence in myself as a martial artist gave me the courage to do such a dangerous thing. Or perhaps it just seemed reasonable to me back then since I'd already been alone with strangers. I was already programmed to trust older white men and look to them for protection, affection, and physical pleasure.

The rest of the summer was a blur. Everything seemed to happen so fast in those days. I spent my last few months sneaking into gay bars with my only gay friend, Joey, who had a crush on me. We were never sexual, but we were the closest of friends. Joey was the first person I could talk to and tell my thoughts to. I guess you could say he was my first "real" friend.

Joey made his money sleeping with older men, but I didn't know it then. At the time, Joey told me he was doing odd jobs for Mr. Chrysler. I often dropped him off at a mansion and waited for him to come out with his usual 100 dollars.

The days and nights flew seamlessly, mainly because we rarely woke up before four or five in the afternoon, and sometimes even as late as six o'clock. But the summer was cut short after my parents found out my sister was not going to school and partying away their money and ordered us both to get in the car and come back to Virginia Beach. Although the summer ended on a bad note, I will always cherish the time I spent in Atlanta because it would be the last time my sister and I were really close.

CHAPTER 19

BOOT CAMP

After the summer with my sister in Atlanta, I started to come out of my shell, learning about the world. But I did have one massive fear, and that was the fear of being discovered. Eventually, I would be forced to face that fear alone.

In the fall, it was time for me to report to the US Army boot camp. I was excited about leaving home and finally being free to be myself. But at the same time, I had this feeling in the back of my mind that I was making a mistake. At the time, none of my friends understood why I joined the Army. Growing up at the beach, we routinely made fun of "navy squids" and anyone in a military uniform.

I remember asking myself if I would be better off going to college. My grades were good enough to get into college, but I was sick of school. What I really wanted was to play table tennis at the 1984 Olympics. According to that slick-talking recruiter my dad had spoken to, the US Army was my ticket to gold and glory. Boy, was I naïve!

It was mid-November, and I had just turned 17 years old. I left home at 4 on a chilly Sunday morning. I still remember entering Fort Knox's iron gates and seeing the long white barracks that looked like something out of a World War II movie. I got a sense of excitement like something great was going to happen. After all, I was a martial artist in the best shape of my life. Heck, I wasn't even 18, and I had already fought two world champions, so the idea of being in the military started to look like something where I could excel.

Like most people, I had no idea what I was in for. The Army looked far more glamorous through the eyes of my favorite WW II movie director, Steven Spielberg. So, in my ignorance, I jumped in with both feet. To be honest, that was my attitude about almost everything. I approached things assuming that I would be the best at whatever I was doing. Like many other traits, I inherited this "winner takes it all" attitude from my father.

My dad had made it his mission to instill the "killer instinct" in me, because as far as he was concerned, I would be a world champion. I hated losing, especially to him, because he would belittle me in front of everyone.

He barely said anything when I won, which made winning all the sweeter. I enjoyed shutting him up as often as I could. I felt tremendous pressure to please my father in those days, and the only way to do that was by winning.

Upon arriving at boot camp, the drill sergeants immediately started to scream and yell at us. They made some guys drop and do hundreds of push-ups for not moving fast enough or not saying "Yes, Sir" loud enough. They cursed and bellowed, calling our mothers "whores" and us "sons of bitches." They also loved calling us "faggots" and "girls" or "ladies." The game was simple: weed out the weak ones through physical exhaustion, humiliation, and intimidation.

Many of the other recruits were visibly frightened by the drill sergeants yelling and screaming at us every second of our waking hours, from sunup to sundown. The drill sergeants were big men, like the older boys and men who had molested me, so I found some of them attractive. I even had a crush on one of them. Consequently, none of their well-rehearsed scare tactics worked on me. I actually liked the way they carried themselves, and I respected them. I was also far too confident as a fighter and far too naïve to realize the trouble I would bring myself for being too cocky.

The weeks flew by like the wind at Fort Knox. Everything was hurried up. So many things happened, so many mistakes as well as many victories. The Army made us men, and I got through the training like a pro, receiving top marks in every area of physical fitness. During the physical fitness test,

I completed the two-mile run in nine minutes. I did over 80 push-ups and 100 sit-ups in one minute flat. My physical abilities were far superior to most of my fellow recruits, and I wasn't afraid to show it.

One night, some of the guys in my platoon decided to play a game of poker. We often played card games to pass the time. One of the guys I secretly had a crush on asked me to join the game. I told them I didn't know how to play, and of course, they said, "No problem, we'll teach you."

I literally didn't know what I was doing, but somehow I managed to win hand after hand. After a few hands, tensions started to rise between me and a Mexican guy, which is understandable since we always played for real money. The military is a gambling culture. Believe me when I tell you, soldiers will bet on anything.

At some point, the guy started to raise his voice and accuse me of cheating, which I laughingly denied. The next thing I knew, the guy jumped up from his chair and took a swing at me. Before he could blink, I had knocked him to the other side of the room with a jump sidekick. He didn't see it coming, and he just lay there on the floor with a stunned look on his face. I stood there in my fighting stance like Bruce Lee in *Enter the Dragon* and suddenly realized the room had gone quiet and everyone was looking at me.

That was the first and last fight I had in the Army. The word of my skills, some of which was greatly exaggerated, spread across the entire base like a California wildfire. My fellow soldiers all looked up to me from that day forward, and I had become somewhat of a celebrity on base.

On the other hand, the drill sergeants, for the most part, didn't think much of me, or maybe they did, and that's why they were always on my back. On more than one occasion, I found myself behind closed doors with two drill sergeants threatening me with bodily harm. I would just laugh. There was a particular drill sergeant from the deep south. He was a big son of bitch, and boy, was he mean. The guy had big bug-like eyes that made him look insane. When he got angry and started to scream, his face would contort like a gorilla's. He constantly threatened me and even hit me on more than one occasion. I took his abuse and most times laughed it off. As far as I was concerned, I was only there to play table tennis and wouldn't have to put up with those losers much longer.

Boot camp, for the most part, was an exciting time for me in the Army. I'd been so isolated and psychologically screwed up from all the years of abuse and the constant moving from one state to the other, from one home to the next. Maybe this is why I wasn't emotionally ready for the choices I would ultimately make at that time of my life. My parents had kept me sheltered, and I had no experience in the real world. I didn't have any real friends before. At boot camp, I finally met some cool people and met a few guys that would become my lifelong friends.

I smoked marijuana for the first time at boot camp. I wanted to be liked and not feared, so three other guys and I went out to the baseball field right before lights out. Luston, the only Hawaiian guy I've met, had a package he called Maui Waui delivered in the mail. I was amazed at the balls he had to have a joint mailed from Hawaii to boot camp just days before graduation. If he had got caught, he'd have been sent to Leavenworth, no questions asked. But he pulled it off, and we smoked the night before graduation in the middle of the badly-lit baseball field across from the barracks.

I remember taking my first puff of the joint and the feeling of my chest tightening as I tried desperately not to cough. Luston and the other guys started laughing. "Watch me," Luston said. I watched him inhale slowly and deeply. He held his breath for about 30 seconds, then slowly blew out a huge cloud of white smoke that smelled like fruity pine trees.

We stopped in the chow hall before returning to the barracks, where I proceeded to devour everything on site. After a few minutes, everything changed. It was as if time and everything around me had suddenly slowed down, and I could not stop laughing. We walked back to the barracks, went inside to the cafeteria, and bought lots and lots of food.

Let me tell you; food never tasted so good. I could not stop eating. I ate two hamburgers, a hot dog, French fries, a pizza slice, and chocolate cake. I don't recall how much time passed before I finally stopped pigging out. I was normal for just a few moments, and then the laughing fit returned, so Luston and the other guy had to take me back to my room. I never felt so happy and free, and I would chase that happy feeling of being high for years to come.

The next day our families and friends came to see us graduate before being shipped off to our individual duty stations. During the big marching ceremony, we impressed our families, showing them the disciplined soldiers we had all been transformed into by good old Uncle Sam and the US Army. But the real fun began when we got our bonus checks for taking up hazardous duty jobs.

I had signed up to be a tank driver, which came with an $8,000 bonus, as the average lifespan of a tank on the battlefield was about 30 seconds. But that didn't matter to me. We weren't at war, and hell, like most soldiers, I thought I was invincible. Besides, I was told that as a tank driver, my duty station would be in Germany, so I could begin my training for the Olympics and even play in the big European leagues. I was so excited!

After cashing my big fat bonus check at the base's Credit Union, I remember my excitement as I tried to put the stack of crisp new one-hundred-dollar bills into my wallet. Quite frankly, I'd never seen so much money in my life. I was on top of the world! Money was something we never spoke about in my family. I was clueless about the value of money. I grew up not always getting what I wanted, and even though I always got what I needed, I felt inferior because all my rich white friends had everything they wanted and more than they needed.

At the end of that glorious day, I kept a promise I made to my mother when I was a kid. I had promised her that one day I'd buy her a mink coat. So, after graduation, I gave her $2000 to buy a mink coat. Boy, was she surprised! I could tell she was so proud of me that day. She even cried a little. But the surprise was all mine later that evening when I received my orders to report to my permanent duty station – Fort Polk, Louisiana.

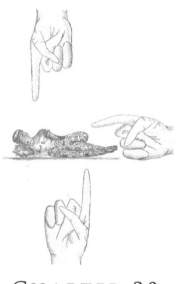

CHAPTER 20

WELCOME TO MY NIGHTMARE: FORT POLK, LOUISIANA

I'd been given two weeks to go home and visit my family and friends before reporting to my duty station. During this time, I also had to buy myself a new car. As I wasn't old enough to actually buy the car from the dealer, my father had to sign for me again.

When I got to the Toyota dealership, I was expecting to drive away in my new, fully automatic Honda Prelude I had asked for. Instead, I got a new Toyota Celica GT with a five-speed automatic transmission that I had no idea how to drive. The next day, after figuring out how to shift gears, I set off for Fort Polk, Louisiana, 3rd & 70th Armored Division.

Fort Polk was a culture shock indeed. Louisiana was as country as it gets. On the first day of orientation, all of the "colored" soldiers were instructed where we could and could not go. We were told to always go in groups and never to visit certain areas alone. This was because the grand wizard of the Ku Klux Klan lived just miles from the base.

My only lifeline was the weekly calls home. We didn't have the magic of cell phones back in 1983. In those days calling home meant standing in line to wait your turn at payphones out in front of the barracks to make a collect call to dear old Mom and Dad. So, I waited in line and made the first of many calls home. As soon as my father picked up the phone, I asked him what I was doing in Louisiana instead of Germany. I screamed, "Why did that Army recruiter guy promise me I was going to Germany?" I was furious and told my father I wanted to go home. He told me not to worry, and it was only temporary. He tried his best to assure me I'd be on my way to Germany before I knew it. He told me to keep training and speak with the base commander, and everything would be fine once they knew who I was and why I was there.

I hung up the phone, and my heart sunk. For the first time, I realized my father, whom I admired and looked up to so much, wasn't perfect. He had been outsmarted by an unscrupulous Army recruiter and unwittingly altered my destiny again.

It was 1983, and the 1984 Olympics were just a year away, so I proceeded to go to my superiors daily about my desire to train and the promises I had been given. However, I would soon realize my pleading fell on deaf ears; in fact, I was literally laughed out of the base commander's office on more than one occasion. Slowly but surely, my frustration and anger continued to grow.

During my time in Fort Polk I made friends with the person who would become my partner in crime and the person who would lead me into the music business. Tevin was a tall, dark-skinned brother from Louisiana. For the most part, he wasn't a bad looking guy, except for the missing front tooth. We originally met in boot camp. He was one of the many fellow soldiers that witnessed my martial arts skills and sort of latched on to me. At Fort Polk, I was assigned to Charlie Company, and Tevin was in Delta Company, but we started to hang out nearly every day.

Something about Tevin and I just clicked. We both shared a love of music, but not just any kind of music. He liked punk rock and new wave. Tevin was the first black guy I'd ever met that liked the same kind of music as I did. He told me he was a drummer, and I lied and told him I could play the bass. We decided to start a band, and we called it Ariel UXL.

We found a place on the base where we could rent instruments and a room to practice. Every day after working in the motor pool, we would eat chow and then buy a six-pack of beer and pretend to be a band. Man, were we terrible! Well, *I* was terrible. Tevin was a great drummer, and I was happy to be in the US Army for a little while.

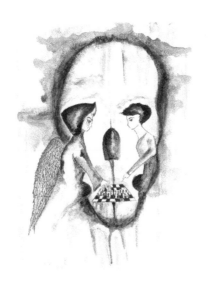

CHAPTER 21

SYMPATHY FOR THE DEVIL

Days passed, then weeks, then months, then a year. It became painfully clear I wasn't going to the Olympics. No one for a hundred miles could play at my level. Therefore, my skills began to fade, and I finally gave up all hope. In the immortal words of my later band, Black Betty, "It was a bitter bite to eat." However, I washed it down with my new obsession of "being in a band" and as many drugs and alcohol as I could get my hands on.

The Army was turning out to be not only a terrible disappointment to me but also a waking nightmare. Consequently, my character continued to change. My clean living and boy scout attitude had turned into a troublemaker, drunkard, and partier.

I decided that God hated me. I asked him why He made me black and gay. I asked him why he smashed my Olympic dreams by sending me to this horrible place. When I got no answers, I started to hate Him, too. I literally didn't give a fuck anymore.

I decided to serve Satan and be as evil as I could be. I met some fellow soldiers with whom I began practicing and studying black magic and Satanism in my room. I even created an altar with magical instruments. I spent all my free time getting high and casting spells and learning about the practice of magic.

I took enough acid and magic mushrooms to fry a normal person's brain completely. I saw strange beings, demons and angels, magic wheels, and fiery dragons soaring across the midnight sky during my acid trips. One night, Tevin and I were in my room tripping on purple microdots so bad that I had to leave the room. It wasn't until the next day that I realized I had walked several miles in my underwear. I had been following a light that led me deep into the woods, and I spent the entire night sitting there without my clothes on, talking to Jesus. I spent the next ten days reading the Bible from cover to cover and telling everyone in my company that Jesus was coming soon.

A few days later, our entire division moved to Fort Irwin in the Southern California desert for war games. We often got high, drunk, and even did acid during these live-fire war games. Looking back now, I realize how crazy and dangerous that behavior was. I could have killed someone or been killed, and I nearly did more than once while driving the 53-ton tank. Once I ran into a huge ditch that caused my tank commander to fall from a torrent and break his arm. I was high on acid and didn't hear his command to turn, even though he had been screaming in my headset. On another occasion, I ran over the guard shack and almost killed the guards inside.

Being in this desert area was the perfect opportunity for me to do the ultimate satanic ritual and invoke my "familiar," a demon that a magician calls upon to help accomplish magical works. I planned everything perfectly. I waited till the moon was perfect and full. While everyone was sleeping in their tents, I snuck out just before midnight with the various magical items I had brought with me to a remote area I had picked out earlier. I waited till the appointed time and drew my magic circle on the ground along with the magical signs for protection, and then began chanting.

After finishing the invocation, I stood there under the light of the bright full moon and waited for a long, long time. I was just about to give up on the whole thing when I looked up into the night sky, and out of nowhere, I saw two enormous black crows appear. I couldn't believe my eyes. The two giant birds flew down and landed just outside my protective circle. They were at least two feet tall, jet black with glowing red eyes. The air around me was completely silent and pitch black, except for the light of the full moon. The two giant black birds spoke to me, not with words but telepathically, just as when I was a kid back at the school for the gifted in San Francisco.

They asked me why I had summoned them here. I said the magical words of protection and then made my request. According to the ritual, I would be allowed three wishes: I wished to have Sergeant Mort fall in love with me, I wished to be famous, and… I paused for a moment. I could feel hatred, something very dark, and I remember being very afraid for a moment. Then I was asked if there was anything else. I said, "Yes, there is. I want to be eternally young." Then they asked me, "What will you give us in return?" This was a powerful magical rite that required a sacrifice. I replied without hesitation, "My soul." "So be it," they said, then they spread their giant black wings and disappeared into the night sky.

As I closed the ritual, I was trying to process everything that had happened. I finished everything just as I had read and was very careful to follow all the instructions. It was fairly late when I returned to camp but, I decided I needed to hit the showers… and the strangest thing happened. When I went to the shower, to my surprise, there he was: Sergeant Mort.

He was a 30-year-old white chubby male from Virginia. He smiled at me and asked, "You're Andrews, right?" I was surprised he knew my name. He stood there naked, and we talked for a while about Dungeons & Dragons, music, and his collection of Beatles records.

I remember being so nervous and thinking, *Wow, maybe the ritual really worked.* Eventually, he got dressed and left, but he invited me to hang out with him when we got back to Fort Polk. I said, "Sure, that would be great." Then I took a shower and returned to my tent and thought nothing of it again.

At this point in my life, I was so confused about everything: my sexuality, my molestations, my family, my career, my dream of going to the Olympics. The countless hours of training had kept all my demons at bay, but I started to realize nothing was going the way I had imagined it. My world, or at least my perception of the world and the people around me, was becoming unbearable.

A lot of my anger was with my parents. Why did they leave me with that babysitter? Why weren't they rich? Why weren't they white? Why did they tell me to join the Army? I started to resent my parents, and I spoke to them less and less. Sometimes even weeks passed without speaking to them. And it wasn't just my parents I resented, but also myself. After I got back from the desert training, my self-hatred had reached its apex, and I wanted to be somebody else. I wanted out of the Army.

CHAPTER 22

NUMBERS

Tevin and I had convinced ourselves we were too cool for the Army; we were rock stars. We went from city to city around Louisiana, looking for that place where we could feel like ourselves. I was the one with the brand-new car, but I remember I always let Tevin drive. He loved driving my car, and I loved letting him drive it because I could get high and drunk and not worry about getting busted for driving under the influence. Every payday, we took our checks and bought new clothes and cassette tapes. The Walkman was like our god. Punk had evolved into new wave and goth, and we started listening to groups like The Cure, Siouxsie and the

Banshees, Bauhaus, and Joy Division. During our trips, Tevin and I had formed a brotherly bond.

One day we heard through word of mouth that Houston, Texas, was the place to party. It was a big city with bars and nightclubs, and one thing I learned that summer I stayed in Atlanta with my sister was that big cities meant gay bars. The very next weekend, we headed out west to Houston. The first couple of times, we took Catcher with us. He was a big cornbread-fed country boy from North Carolina. He was thick all over; he looked like a football lineman. I was very attracted to him, but I never showed it. I was still terrified and pretending to be straight.

Every weekend for months, we drove my bright red Celica west to find a place that looked "cool" enough for us to hang out and party. We had it down to a science. We always pretended to be in a band. Tevin and I were the artists, and Catcher was our manager. The story was always the same. We were coming off tour and decided to drive back to LA because we wanted to stop at a few places and party with the locals. Our manager was here to keep us out of trouble and make sure we made it back to LA in time for the Grammys or a recording session or whatever.

Big old Catcher, who was a mountain of a man, would go to the door and start talking with that country drawl, and somehow, we would be escorted through the door and ushered straight to the VIP section. It worked like a charm every time. God bless him. I still can't believe people actually believed us. We had people coming over to us asking for our autographs and buying us rounds of shots. I actually felt sorry for one DJ who kept apologizing because he couldn't find our record. He even bought us a bottle of expensive champagne and announced us over the PA as VIP guests of the club.

Then during one magical acid trip, Tevin and I stumbled on a street called Westheimer. I don't remember how we found it, but it was like finding heaven. And right on the strip of Westheimer, we found a bar called Numbers that would be our temple of the gods of music for the next year.

Westheimer Street was the hippest, most exciting place in Houston for an eighteen-year-old kid with nothing but money to burn. It was a mixture of pool halls, gays bars, drag bars, leather bars, bookstores, and, of course, IHOPs and taco bars. But wait, there's more. Just one block over was Montrose Street. It catered to those seeking unrestrained seduction and mayhem. A short walk down Montrose, one knew instantly they were getting the full monty. There was nothing but seedy massage parlors, sex clubs, gay leather bars, drug dealers, and down dark alleyways, hookers of every shape and size.

There were cops everywhere, but no one ever seemed to care. In fact, the cops were just as much a part of the scene as anyone else. People from every walk of life frequented the street, 6-foot-tall drag queens in 6-inch heels, butch lesbians on motorcycles, black dudes selling weed, Mexicans selling cocaine, heroin addicts looking to score, rich kids showing off the car Daddy bought them, bikers and low riders, and of course us, the club kids. It's hard to believe now how cool it really was back then.

We were regulars at Numbers. Back then, it didn't matter if you were gay, straight, a goth, punk, new romantic, new waver, hell, we were even cool with new hip hop kids who sometimes came to Numbers to breakdance. I'd finally found people like me, who wore makeup and dressed in black, and everyone did drugs. We did acid, mushrooms, or ecstasy, and most of the time, all three every weekend. It was like I had died and gone to heaven, a place I could escape my Army prison.

Going to Numbers became our obsession. As soon as we got off on Friday, unless we had guard duty or were in the field, we packed our bags and drove to Houston. The first few times, we slept in my car after being out all night. It never occurred to us that we could just get a hotel.

It wasn't long before some of the other guys wanted to know what the big deal with Houston, Texas was and asked if they could tag along. On a couple of those trips, a black guy named Tony also came with us. One night, we went to a gay bar called Lola's, and I caught Tony kissing a guy. He was afraid I would tell, but I told him not to worry, because I was gay too. We laughed and never spoke of it again.

On the way back, we were hit by a drunk driver that totaled the car we were driving. Thank God that was the one time we didn't take my car. People stopped going to Houston with Tevin and me after the car accident. We, however, continued to go until a strange thing happened after coming back from Houston.

It was Sunday night, not too late in the evening. I dropped Tevin off and was coming up the stairs of my barracks. As I was passing down the hallway, I saw a door open, and inside there were a bunch of fellows playing Dungeons & Dragons and drinking beers. Sergeant Mort was also in the room. He gave me a big welcoming smile and said, "Andrews, hey, buddy." He had a bit of a country accent that sounded a little more educated than the typical redneck. I guess he was what we'd call a geek by today's definitions.

He was chubby but solid as a horse. He wore glasses and had dark brown hair and blue eyes that were always bright and welcoming. I said hello to everyone and started to walk down the walkway. He stopped me and asked me if I wanted to go up to his room and play some video games. I said, "Sure, sounds like fun." Mario Bros was the new big thing at that time, and Sergeant Mort was the only one that actually had a game console.

The next thing I know, we are heading up the stairs together, and he is smiling, and I'm actually feeling nervous like I always feel when I get around someone that I find attractive. Before I could react, he picks me up and carries me the rest of the way to his room. I was about 138 lbs and 5'9" and Sargent Mort was a good 220 lbs and 6 ft.

In his room, he sat down right next to me on his bunk, looked into my eyes, and explained that his roommate was gone for the weekend. The next thing I know, he was telling me he was in love with me and didn't know how to love me, but he wanted to learn. Before I knew it, he leaned over and kissed me. One thing led to another, and soon we were naked in his bunk having sex.

In the morning, I snuck back down to my room. I lay in my bunk listening to my roommate snore, thinking about Sergeant Mort and what had just happened. I couldn't believe it. A sergeant who was supposedly straight and whom I'd spoken to only in passing had fallen in love with me. Did the spell work? It couldn't have been a coincidence. That's when I started to believe in magic and the power of belief.

The next two weeks were like heaven on earth. Sergeant Mort and I fell deeply in love. We spent every possible moment together, sneaking around after work to meet at a hotel or take a drive and just hold hands and talk about our future together. He gave me flowers and mixtapes of love songs by the Beatles. It was like a dream come true. But like all black magic, I had a karmic debt to pay.

One night, Sergeant Mort came to my room. He told me he couldn't stop thinking about me and he had to see me. I let him in my room because my roommate, a super cool black guy from New York, told me he would be gone for the weekend with his girlfriend.

It started with just talking about life and music and how we felt about each other. Then it progressed to holding hands and kissing, then hugging and embracing till we found ourselves under the covers in the throes of passion. As Sergeant Mort was reaching his peak, he became very verbal. Then I heard a noise. Before either of us could react, there was my roommate, standing in the door with a look on his face I don't think I will ever forget. I couldn't begin to imagine what was going through his head.

There I was, legs in the air with Sergeant Mort literally on top of me, butt naked and sweating. I tried to bury my face, but it was too late. My roommate turned and ran out the door. To say we freaked out is a massive understatement. We were fucked, and we knew it.

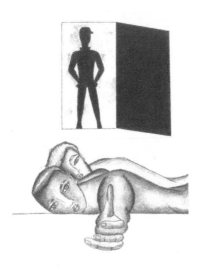

CHAPTER 23

DON'T ASK, DON'T TELL

We got dressed in a total and complete panic, never speaking or even looking at one another. We looked around and dashed down the stairs to Sergeant Mort's car. I cried and cried. We drove all night, clenching one another's hands as we drove down the dark highway till dawn. I had never been so frightened in my life. This was my nightmare come true. We decided we had no choice but to deny everything. So, after we returned to the barracks, we tried our best to get back to our rooms undetected.

When I returned to my room, my roommate and all his belongings were gone. I tried not to panic and got dressed for morning PT (physical training). When I entered the main hall, the room went silent, and upon the chalkboard, a message written in giant letters read, "ANDREWS IS A FAGGOT."

I began shouting and threatening my roommate. My eyes must have been filled with rage because I could see the fear in his eyes as I leaped forward at him, intending to tear him apart. Fortunately for us both, before I reached him, several of the officers present jumped on me and stopped me from reaching him.

As you might imagine, things only got worse for me after that display. I was immediately escorted to the captain's office with my platoon sergeant. I was interrogated over and over for days: "Your roommate said he walked in on you and Sergeant Mort. Did this really happen? Are gay?" I couldn't believe what was happening. My mind was numb. I did my best to stay cool and denied everything. I repeated over and over, "I am not gay. I am not gay."

After some time, Captain Jebb, who I suspected might have been gay himself, finally said he believed my story. However, for my own safety, he was transferring me to another platoon. My roommate was also transferred to another division to prevent any further incidence between him and me. I never saw him again.

I was pretty much segregated from the rest of my platoon and company. I was put in a room by myself, with no roommates. I was not allowed to see Sergeant Mort. I was crying and freaking out. No one would sit by me in the chow hall or the training room. I couldn't talk to anyone. It was overwhelming. In desperation, I went to Tony, the kid I saw kissing another guy at the bar in Houston.

I had written a letter to Sergeant Mort telling him that I loved him and that I would leave with him if he left. I gave the letter to Tony, who gave me his word he would not show it to anyone or read it before delivering it to Sergeant Mort. I was a fool to believe him.

The next day I was the laughingstock of the entire battalion. Tony went and showed my letter to everyone. Sergeant Mort was busted down to a private, and a week later, he was kicked out with a dishonorable discharge. I was not allowed to see him. I was completely and utterly devastated. Through it all, I continued to deny writing the letter. I claimed Tony did it to be a dick because I threatened to kick his butt. Some people, eventually, believed me, others didn't.

I was still the same person, but because I was now "gay," everyone and everything around me changed, mostly for the worse. I was not getting along with my superiors. As far as I was concerned, they were a bunch of hillbilly rednecks and country ass negros. I despised them, and they felt the same about me. I challenged them at every chance I got. They called me a smart-ass know-it-all spoiled rich boy, which surprised me because my family was far from rich. Being in the Army and "being all you could be" had become a brutal nightmare for me because once the sergeants don't like you, they are gunning for you. They constantly joked behind my back.

Let me tell you, during my time in the Army, I was assaulted by a sergeant on more than one occasion. I was in a beer tent in Germany, we were there for a 6-month training exercise, and this sergeant put a bowie knife to my throat. Everyone saw the incident, but when I went to the captain to complain, no one admitted that they had seen it.

Everything came to a boiling point after being placed on KP (kitchen detail) for the millionth time while we were out in the "field," aka "the swamps of Louisiana." I was standing in the middle of the woods in the rain with a scrubber and a giant metal tub, washing dishes for the entire company, about 300 soldiers, breakfast, lunch, and dinner. I couldn't take it anymore, so I traded a fuel truck driver I knew for a joint to take me back to the rear. It was a huge risk, but he went for it. I hid under the dash, and he drove me back to the headquarters.

When I got back to my room, it was clear there was no turning back. Leaving the field without permission was a serious offense. In military terms, it's called "going AWOL." Deserting the field meant a court-martial and possible time in the Leavenworth military prison. But I didn't care anymore. Being in prison would be better than staying in the Army.

When I got to my room, I found Sergeant Rockington, my new roommate, there with a broken arm, which kept him from going to the field. He had broken it driving us to Atlanta the month before. He had fallen asleep at the wheel and flipped the car over on I-95. We were lucky to be alive to talk about it.

As soon as I walked in the room, he asked, "Hey, Andrews, aren't you supposed to be in the field?" But then he stopped me before I could reply, saying, "I don't want to know, but whatever you do, don't come back, or they are going to put you in jail this time." I looked him in the eye and shook his hand. I was sure that would be the last time I'd see him.

I got my car loaded with my things as fast as possible. As I was about to leave, Tevin walked up and said, "Hey, Andrews, where you are going? Aren't you supposed to be in the field?"

I quickly explained what had happened, just how fed up I was and how I couldn't do it anymore. To my surprise, Tevin said he was going with me. He said we were brothers, and he wasn't going to let me go alone. I hugged him and tried my best not to cry. We hurried and got his things.

Since we were in the middle of the field exercises, the base was like a ghost town—the perfect time to make our escape. We didn't say, but we knew exactly where we were going. We were heading to Houston, Texas. I gave Tevin the keys and jumped in the passenger seat. Even after all the car accidents and near-death experiences traveling from city to city the past two years, I still didn't think about buckling my seat belt.

My red Celica had everything, except for the one thing I really wanted, a cassette player. Thank God Tevin had a killer ghetto blaster that we propped up in the back window. We blasted the Cure and Siouxsie and the Banshees as we rode through the main gate, right past security. We even made a stop at the base liquor store, then we drank beer and bottles of Boone's Farm until we got to a small town right before the Louisiana-Texas border.

I remember feeling that this was a big mistake, but it was too late. I'd ruined my life, and there was no turning back. I thought about my mom and dad and my sister and wondered if I'd ever see them again. I wanted to call them and say goodbye, but I didn't want to talk to my mom. Somehow, she could always tell when something was wrong, and I didn't want her to talk me out of it. Thankfully, the feeling quickly passed, and we sang along to Depeche Mode, Dead or Alive, and The Cult.

We soon realized we didn't have any drugs on us. Luckily, one of the many skills I developed in the Army was how to spot where to find drugs. It's an art form, really, and I just happen to excel at finding "where da weed at." But, in this case, we were obviously in a hurry to get out of Louisiana. We were constantly looking back, waiting to hear a siren from the military police or maybe even the state troopers or Texas Rangers.

We drove around and found the hood with some homeboys posted on the block. I rolled down the window and asked for the stuff, and the guy handed me an ounce. Just as I was going to hand the guy the money, another guy comes from around the back with a gun pointing towards us. Tevin had been watching the rearview, and before the guy could get to the side window, Tevin popped the car into reverse, knocking the guy off his feet. He slammed the gear shift into first and peeled out of that shady neighborhood like Evil Knievel.

The drug dealers didn't give up that easily. Believe it or not, they jumped in a car and followed us almost all the way to the Texas border until they finally turned around. We laughed our butts off and celebrated our victory by smoking a huge joint made from our free bag of Mexican weed.

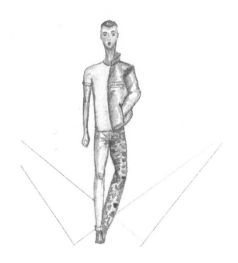

CHAPTER 24

HOUSTON GOES TO HOUSTON

I had made this trip every weekend since we first discovered Numbers. The lure of the city, the sex, drugs, and of course the music – it's always about the music! – possessed my heart and soul. Looking back, it's probably the real reason why I went AWOL; not because I wanted out of the Army so much as I wanted to escape my past and become somebody new. And where better than Houston, Texas? I remember the feeling I would get every time I saw the city's skyline coming over the horizon as we approached. We would immediately turn the music up even louder, light up another joint, and take a shot of whatever we had in a brown paper bag. We both always would suddenly come alive with this feeling of joy and excitement when we saw the Houston skyline. All my troubles and worries about the Army melted away: As far as I was concerned I was done with the fucking Army, and I wasn't going back alive. That was what I was telling myself that as we got off the exit and headed to the strip.

For the first few days or maybe a week, we lived out of my car and crashed with friends and sometimes strangers we met at parties. We had created a whole new identity for ourselves. I left anything that might connect me to the Army behind, except for my dress uniform and my very punk rock tanker boots, which were my pride and joy.

We kept up the story that we were in a band and that we had a record deal. It also explained the seemingly deep pockets we had and the amazing clothes we had bought in Germany. Everyone believed everything I said. I was getting very good at creating stories.

After a couple of weeks, we found an apartment in the local "fag rag" called TWT. It was not just any apartment, but an apartment within a complex near The Galleria. The Galleria was Houston's pride at that time, a fabulous high-end mall filled with trendy shops and endless cruising in the bathroom stalls. It was perfect. What better way to escape the military than hiding out in a gay apartment complex, where the tenants, manager, staff, and owners were all gay? Every Sunday, they had a beer bust by the pool, and literally, every night was a party. They would never think of looking for us there.

We paid our first three months' rent in advance with the money from our final check from our original bonus money. However, we first had to get that money. I had balls of steel in those days. After being AWOL for a good three weeks knowing that the military and local police had warrants on us, we decided to drive back to the base and go to the company headquarters to sign our last bonus check. I still can't believe we got away with it.

We drove 145 miles from Houston to Fort Polk. At the military base, Tevin and I strolled into headquarters and showed our IDs to get our checks. Believe it or not, they gave us the money! Two grand apiece. We got in the car and made it back to Houston with pockets full of cash to buy records, clothes, drugs, booze, and accessories. It was clear that I was born under a lucky star.

CHAPTER 25

CLUB KIDS

We became regulars on the Houston nightclub strip. A small group of us were known for only wearing black and doing copious amounts of acid. We called ourselves "the witches" because one of our favorite things to do on the dance floor was forming a circle and dancing like witches whenever certain songs came on. Music had become my new god. It was a pantheon of immortal bands that I worshipped: The Cure, Depeche Mode, The Smiths, New Order, Dead or Alive, and David Bowie. I was into anything underground and anti-establishment. The darker, the better. The nights were magical, and I waded through them like a dream.

We mimicked our musical heroes in every way we could. We copied everything from the clothing they wore to the way they spoke on the video interviews we would watch endlessly. I even permed my hair straight and dyed it blue and black to look more like Siouxsie. I wore dresses, earrings, and makeup; I tried my best to be completely androgynous in those days.

I had a set routine on the weekends that consisted of starting our nights at Lola's, a dive pick-up bar about a block or so away from Numbers. Lola's offered 10-cent drinks for happy hour, and it was the perfect place to begin our night. Then we were off to JR's or what we liked to call the Polo Lounge. JR's was where all of the rich queens and polo twinks went for cheap drinks before going on to one of the bigger clubs.

There was a particular night that my acid was kicking in hard. I was feeling overwhelmed by the lights and sounds and strange faces exploding all around me. So, to get some relief from the heavy acid trip, I decided to go outside to get some fresh air. I wandered around for a while and came upon a place called The Drum.

The Drum was the next level of gaydom that I had never experienced before. It was an out-of-the-way bar tucked away in a poorly lit corner. What caught my attention was the very "manly- looking" men going in and out of the place. I had to investigate. As I walked up to the door, I was stopped by a huge, burly-looking bouncer. He looked at my typical androgynous all-black goth club kid outfit and said, "You can't come in unless you are wearing leather or blue jeans."

Without hesitating, I asked, "Okay, where can I buy some leather?" He didn't say a word but lifted his arm and pointed to a shop across the street. I looked at the shop, then I looked back at him and said, "I'll be right back." Fifteen minutes later, I was standing in front of the guy, wearing a pair of $200 leather jeans. This time, he let me in, and he never bothered to ask me for my ID. I was 19 years old and was about to discover the underground world of gay leather, bondage, and S&M.

I was in a very dark place at this point in my life. I was living day to day in terror of being arrested at any moment for being AWOL from the Army. My molesters had taught me to seek sex for comfort and attention. I was a lamb before the slaughter, and Houston was full of older gay/bi and straight men preying on "fresh meat" like me.

Just walking into The Drum was sensory overload. Men were everywhere dressed in leather and ass-less chaps, jockstraps, and some wearing nothing at all. There was even a sex shop in the club. These men were like football players, bodybuilders, and stocky, hairy men. It was the exact opposite of JR's. There were pool tables and slings and porn videos playing on every TV monitor. The music was underground with a deep bass sound and driving beat.

At the very back of the bar was a door covered by a black curtain, which had a red light bulb over the doorway. I could see men going in and out of the black curtains all night. At some point, after a few vodkas, I decided to follow one big daddy bear guy who'd checked me out from across the bar into the black curtained dark room.

The curtained doorway led to a maze of rooms filled with men having sex in all manner of ways. I dove headfirst into that dark world and found myself seeking other dark places like the gay men's saunas and bathhouses. I found myself involved in one sexual situation after another with strangers, most of whom I never spoke to or knew their names. I knew in my heart that I was ruining my life. I knew that sooner or later I was going to get caught.

Because every day was a pre-party and every night was a party (and every morning the after-party), Tevin and I were soon running out of money. We couldn't risk going back to the base anymore to cash checks. We had no choice. We had to find work. The question was, What sort of jobs could we possibly get without alerting the Army and the police of our whereabouts?

Then one of us had a great idea. We could be escorts. We were acquainted with a guy named Calder, no last name, just Calder. He was an escort and virtually a celebrity around town. He was a beautiful man, tall and thin, with striking features and long blonde hair. Everyone seemed to know him. He wore the most fabulous outfits and drove a brand-new cherry red Alfa Romeo Spider. I was completely fascinated with how free and together he always seemed to be. He presented himself as a carefree person, always smiling and laughing without a care in the world. His life looked magical from where I was sitting.

Calder referred me to his agency, and I scheduled an interview. Things were going well at first, but near the end of the interview, the escort agent asked me if I had any questions. I asked how much I would earn. She surprised me by saying $300 a date. I was excited at that prospect. Then I asked her one more question: "If I don't like the person, do I have to sleep with them?" She said, "Yes, of course, darling."

That was the end of the interview as far as I was concerned. I could not imagine having sex with skinny guys. You see, my babysitter imprinted a body type on me, and that wasn't going to change so easily. Tevin also backed out because he said he didn't want to get involved with some "weird gay sex drama."

One of our friends, however, did take the job. Tevin and I were blown away because our friend had always said he was straight. Several days later, he got a call for a date. Later that night, as we were standing in front of Numbers with a few friends getting high and tripping on acid, a long, black limo pulled up. The back door opened, and our friend hopped out and walked towards us. He looked as if he'd just seen a ghost. We asked him what happened on the date. He said he didn't want to talk about it, but it was the last time he would escort. We took that money and partied for days.

CHAPTER 26

STREET FIGHTER

It was a typical Friday night, and we were hanging out in front of Numbers as we always did. Tevin and I were tripping hard on some excellent acid. Earlier in the evening, we sat in my car, watching *The Flintstones* and zooming down the road until I rolled down my window and realized we had been sitting in the parking lot the entire time, experiencing some simultaneous hallucination on the brick wall we were facing. We got out of the car thinking it would be a good idea to go hang out in front of the club with the usual crowd of club kids, drag queens, fag hags, punks, and goth kids that were the "cool" people at Numbers.

I ran into a guy out front who said he had a joint for sale. Back then, joints were cheap, and I just happened to have a fake $5 bill that was folded up so you could only see on the side of it. Some street Christian had given it to me earlier in the evening, and when you opened it up, it said "Jesus loves you." I gave the guy the fake five-dollar bill, and he gave me a fake joint. As soon as I inhaled, I realized it wasn't weed but oregano. Fair enough. We were all so high at that point that everything was funny to us.

But before I knew it, what I thought was no big deal turned ugly real fast. The guy who sold me the fake weed returned and was in front of me holding a switchblade. I wasn't afraid at all and kept on laughing. The people around me were starting to freak out as the guy continued to threaten me, rambling on about how I had somehow ripped him off. I told him to let it go. "We had both ripped each other off. Let's just call it even," I said. He got even angrier and shouted racist names at me.

Everything happened in what seemed like seconds. As the guy went on about me giving him his money, out of the corner of my dilated pupils, I noticed a long metal pipe lying on the ground near the wall . Before he could react, I quickly picked up the four-foot pipe, which made a perfect weapon in my well-trained hands. The whole thing seemed like I was watching a cartoon or a kung fu movie as my acid trip swirled my mind in and out of reality.

The guy backed up, and to everyone's amusement, he whined, "That's not fair. You have a pipe." I burst out laughing, and so did everyone standing around watching the drama that was unfolding. For some reason, I told the guy that if he wanted to go and get a pipe to make it a fair fight to get on, and I'd wait for him right here. I figure that was at that moment I decided to get serious. Moments later, the guy was running back from across the street with a pool stick in his hands and came directly for me. He raised his pool stick and swung it at me with all his might.

My years of training made my reaction quick and totally without thinking. I executed the perfect block and stance and immediately threw several counterstrikes with deadly force. The first strike hit the guy directly across his cheek and temple. I could hear his bones cracking as I stepped to the side and watched him topple over in front of me.

I landed another blow directly across his back, sending him to the ground fast and hard. I stood there frozen in place for I don't know how long. Suddenly, I felt totally sober, and my mind was struggling to cope with what was happening on the ground in front of me. Blood was coming out the side of his head like the Mississippi River. And the worst part was that he wasn't moving. I looked up, and everyone was staring at me. Then I heard Tevin, who was suddenly standing next to me, scream, "Run, Houston, run." And without another thought, I started to run as I'd never run before.

I ran straight through the parking lot like the Flash, turned down the back alley behind Numbers, and headed for The Drum. I knew that no one would look for me there. I was freaking out badly. I saw my whole life flashing before my eyes. After I got to The Drum, I sat at the bar drinking one vodka tonic after another until about 4 am.

As reality set in, I knew I had no choice but to go back to the club because my car was in the parking lot, and Tevin depended on me to get home. When I got there, Tevin and a few others were waiting for me by my car. They told me the police came and the guy was taken away in an ambulance. The witnesses blamed the fight on Bollywood, a black guy who actually looked like me.

After the fight, believe it or not, I was hailed as a hero by my fellow club kids. I became a legendary contributor to Numbers' folklore for months. I was never carded and charged to go into the club again after that night. And many people I didn't even know would just walk up to me and give me free drugs. The fight had elevated my status. I felt a little guilty about getting so much personal pleasure from being recognized for something so outlandish, but I loved the attention.

CHAPTER 27

THE LAST MAN STANDING

Our friend Flip was a typical trendy white upper-middle-class Texas party-till-you-drop kind of guy. He had black hair, blue eyes, and a great haircut. He had invited us back to his house to hang out and continue the party. That night Flip was tripping like a madman. He was driving at 120 miles an hour down the highway that had a speed limit of 70. He had the latest Japanese sports car with a custom stereo system and a blue neon light kit under the car. The car looked like an alien spaceship hovering just above the road and moving at the speed of light as we rocketed around Houston's Texas loop. It took us 30-45 minutes of driving to realize we had been driving in circles around the loop because we were so high that we kept missing out on the exit.

Tip lived with his father, a double amputee due to diabetes. As we drove into the driveway of Flip's parent's home, he told us we didn't need to worry about his father waking up and ruining the party, because he had knocked him out earlier by giving him a half gallon of ice cream. He continued to elaborate how, after his father passed out from diabetic shock, he helped himself to his father's car keys and the liquor cabinet's keys. Finally, he removed his father's hearing aids before putting him to bed.

As you might expect, that was music to our drunken ears. And so, the partying continued. At some point, as fate would have it, I was offered a handful of mushrooms. Without thinking, I took them all, which wasn't the best idea. Mushrooms tend to enhance your perceptions and pull out the deep feeling when you take them. And unfortunately, at the time, I was again in a very dark place.

The acid trip, along with the mushrooms, ecstasy, weed, vodka, and assorted imported beers, sent me over the edge emotionally and mentally that night. I'd reached my breaking point. All my emotions came crashing down on me. Before I could stop myself, I called my mom and dad, who ultimately convinced me to go back to Fort Polk and turn myself in to the base commander, whom my mother and father had been in communication with the entire time I was AWOL.

Sometime in the early morning, just before dawn, Tevin and I arrived at the company headquarters. It was a typical hot and humid Louisiana morning. Mosquitoes were buzzing around, looking for any exposed body area to sink their teeth into. The rest of the battalion was still asleep, and the auto lamps that lit up the grounds were starting to dim.

We sat in the car for close to an hour after we pulled into the parking lot. We were still dressed in our club-kid outfit. I had blue permed hair shaved on one side and earrings, which were against the military dress code. I was wearing a black dress and combat boots along with eyeliner, lipstick, and several crosses on my neck. I had even painted my fingernails black. By military standards, I looked completely insane.

We knew we were fucked, and worst of all, we knew we were probably going to jail, or at the very least, we'd be kicked out of the Army with dishonorable discharges. We looked at each other one last time before getting out of the car. I think we might even have cried a little. I took a long deep breath, then slowly exhaled and prepared to face whatever was waiting for me once I walked into headquarters and back under the control of the Army.

We reported to the duty officer and turned ourselves in. What happened that morning and even the next few days after that are a blur. My name had once again become the talk of the battalion. Naturally, no one could believe I had the audacity to come back. Most of them thought they would never see me again. Some even thought I had left the country and fled to Canada or Mexico, or somewhere in Europe.

A week later, I was court-martialed. Surprisingly enough, it was quick and relatively painless as far as I was concerned. I pleaded guilty and was reduced down in rank from E-3 to E-1, fined $600, and sentenced to 45 days extra duty and restriction to the base, which meant I couldn't leave my barracks unless I was on duty or going to the chow hall.

Unfortunately, Tevin did not receive the same punishment. Just like Sergeant Mort, Tevin was booted from the army with a dishonorable discharge. Yet another person I cared about was hurt because of me. But what was worse was that I was alone again.

The days and months to come were some of the darkest days in my memory. I again found myself possessed by the very demons I had aligned with that night in the desert. I became more and more obsessed with the occult, read many books, and attempted conjuring spells, some of which were successful and some that were not. I had embraced the philosophy of Anton LaVey and his Church of Satanism.

That was my state of mind the day Captain Jebb called me into his office. I sat down, and he asked me if I wanted out of the Army. I quickly replied, "Yes, sir, I do," and started to cry.

He said nothing at first and then very quietly said, "I'm going to do you a favor, Andrews, because I like you. You're a good soldier when you're in the field, but I got the feeling that if you stay here any longer, you're going to force me to put you in jail, and I don't want to do that."

A few days later, I was signing paperwork for my release from the military. I was given a general "under honorable conditions" discharge. I said my goodbyes and thanked Captain Jebb, and before the sunset, I was on a plane heading back home to Virginia.

My arrival at Norfolk Airport was a major shock for my parents, to say the least. I was coming home in shame, having been discharged one year before my scheduled separation date. As I came up the jetway onto the concourse, I could see the look of shock and horror at what they saw. Three years in the Army had transformed me from their innocent little boy into something and someone they did not recognize.

For me, it seemed like returning to Virginia Beach was the beginning of the end of my once great relationship with my parents. Before I left home, as far as they were concerned, I was an angel. I was their perfect son and their favorite child. In my parents' eyes, I was still a born-again Christian. As far as they knew, I didn't drink or do drugs, I was a virgin, I was obedient, I was intelligent, and I was straight. But in reality, I had become a Satanist, I was an alcoholic drug addict, I was a sex addict, I was in total rebellion, and I had done unspeakable things to people and myself.

I was wearing all black; a black sweater with red trim around the neck and sleeves, hoop earrings, a crucifix hanging low around my neck, black eyeliner, and straight permed hair. My mother later said she was frightened by my appearance. She said she could see spirits and demons around me.

It was 1985. I was barely 20 years old, but I felt like my life was over and a complete failure. I had done and seen things from a whole other side of life. And one thing was certain: there was no way I could go back to being who I was when I left Virginia Beach three years ago.

However, I still couldn't admit to my parents that I was gay, nor that I no longer believed in their God. I just stopped going to church. I remember the first Sunday that I decided not to go. My mother kept calling my name, as she so often did and still does when she wants me. I just pretended not to hear her until finally my father came into my room and asked me why I wasn't dressed. I told him I wasn't going. He looked at me for a moment or so, then walked out. They never asked me to go to church again.

I was nevertheless happy to be back home, as in the meantime Tevin had also moved to Virginia Beach. After he was kicked out of the Army, his parents told him he was a disgrace and that he could not come home. It turns out Tevin's father was a big-time Marine officer and a real hard ass. I somehow convinced my mother and father to let Tevin come to Virginia Beach and stay with them in my room until he found his own place. Looking back, I was surprised they said yes.

On the ride home from the airport, I got an earful of the whole story and just how terrible Tevin was behaving, working in a bar, sleeping all day, staying out all night, and coming in drunk every night. My mother pushed my father to ask Tevin to leave eventually.

Tevin and I decided to meet after he got off work down at the beach. I remember being so excited to see Tevin, my brother, and my partner in crime. I romanticized the situation far beyond reality: because of my allegiance with the dark side, magic had worked and had gotten us out of the Army. It landed him in Virginia Beach so that we could fulfill our destiny and form a great band. I guess you could say I was having delusions of grandeur.

To my surprise, I quickly discovered Tevin had joined a punk band called Elvis In Hell. They were pretty good. I remember going to rehearsals with Tevin thinking there would be a place for me in the band. But for some reason, Tevin had turned cold towards me, and I didn't understand why. Instead of becoming part of the band, I found myself being treated like a groupie.

This, of course, began to upset me. I began to feel betrayed. One night before one of their shows, I finally approached Tevin backstage and asked him what happened to us forming our own band like we had always talked about. I remember he laughed at me and asked, "Well, you can barely play the bass. Why would I want to be in a band with you?"

That night during their performance, I walked into the middle of the crowd with revenge on my mind. I decided to use the band's and their fans' energy to cast a powerful spell to destroy the band and give me the power to create a bigger, better band of my own and succeed in the music business.

I stood there in the middle of the crowd and began chanting the magical invocation. I remember feeling the power rising all around. I could see the faces of people around me on the dance floor. I'm sure they were wondering what the heck this guy was doing. At the height of the music, I raised both arms and released a wave of hatred toward the band, especially toward the person I once called brother. I left without saying a word.

1985 was a blur to me. I spent my time back in Virginia Beach, going out nearly daily. I saw several men, one of which would turn out to be the uncle of one of my future famous clients. But something else happened during that time that was more profound, and I believe it had a further impact on my downward spiral.

Sergeant Mort, my first real reciprocal love, called me one day out of the blue. He and his family, who were originally from Pennsylvania, had relocated to Portsmouth, one of the seven cities in the Tidewater area. He had literally moved 20 minutes away from my home in Virginia Beach. It was such good news.

At first, I thought all would be well, and it seemed we were still madly in love. He read my poems, and we spent several days together. But one day, he decided that it was time for me to meet his family and invited me over for dinner. It turned out to be a huge mistake. His mother told me right there at the table that I was not welcome in their home, because I had ruined her son's life by seducing him, turning him into a homosexual, and ruining his army career. She told me to leave.

Sergeant Mort just sat there and said nothing, so I quietly got up from the table and left. That was the last time I saw him. I tried to contact him several times, but he would never come to the phone until finally I was told he didn't want to speak to me and asked that I stop calling him.

I was more than brokenhearted and went on a rampage sleeping with a different guy almost every night. I turned to my old friends for drugs and alcohol to hide my pain. Tevin and I were still friends but nowhere near as close as we were before. I know a lot of that distance came from my jealousy of how well his band was doing.

I had become a regular at the gay bars in Norfolk. There were several gay bars in the Tidewater area, and there were at least ten, maybe even fifteen bars I could frequent: Don't Tell Momma, Nexus, Nutty Buddy's (the black gay bar), Hersey Bar for Lesbians, The Garage (the sleaziest place in town that served the strongest drinks I've ever had to this day), The Q Club, the Boathouse, and the king of all bars, the Late Show. The Late

Show was where I had my first of soon to be many encounters with the police.

But what changed the most that year was that my father retired from the Navy, after which my parents decided to move back to Lubbock, Texas. They asked me to move there with them and enroll at Texas Tech University to get my life back on track. This seemed like a logical path for me at the time. But before we left, something unexpected happened that would affect our relationship forever.

I remember coming home the day before we were leaving for Texas. I walked up to the house, put the key into the lock, and just as I was opening the front door, my mother was standing there holding a letter in her hands. Her eyes were filled with tears. Puzzled and concerned, I asked what was wrong.

That's when she dropped the bomb on me. She said she had been praying because she felt something was wrong, and the Lord told her to go to the mailbox and open my mail. She discovered a letter from a lawyer from Galveston, Texas, who I had met in a bar in Houston. We spent only one weekend together, and I hadn't heard from him since I left Texas.

My Mom stood there, tears running down her face, and asked me if I was a homosexual. I didn't know how to reply. At first, all I could think of was to ask, "God told you to break the law and open my mail?" That evening I was forced to sit at the dining room table for hours while my mother and father heaped hot coals of fire and brimstone on my head. They told me over and over that my lifestyle could only come from the "pit of hell." I can still hear my parents saying a demon of homosexuality possessed me.

This was the first of many times my mother would curse me. She looked at me and actually told me she would pray that nothing would go right for me until I gave up my unholy lifestyle. They told me I had *chosen* that lifestyle. It became their mantra. My father said to me, "How can you be gay? You were a black belt... Why would you choose that life?" My first response was, "I'm still the same person." My second response was, "Dad, why would I *choose* to be black and gay? That puts me at the bottom of the totem pole in America."

It all felt so unfair, so I decided it was time to tell them for the first time ever about my molestation. They were devastated. It was the first and the last time I ever saw my father cry. But then they became angry and started drilling me with questions about why I never told them about being molested before. I told them that I was afraid to speak about it. I was afraid they wouldn't love me anymore if they knew.

The next few weeks were like being a rat in a cage. My mother told everyone at the church I was gay. Preacher after preacher came to the house to pray over me and anoint me with holy oil. I got hit on the head by preachers during that time more than George Foreman did while fighting Ali. They prayed and spoke in tongues and shouted hallelujah and exorcised demon after demon from me.

Meanwhile, I was wrestling with real demons. You see, there was a price to pay for calling whatever that was I conjured up in the desert. It was after me, and it wasn't going to let me go. I couldn't sleep at night. My dreams were horrible nightmares, and I dreaded going to sleep. I cast spell after spell, trying to stop whatever was happening to me and to blind my mother from seeing what was going on. I knew God spoke to her, so I had to keep magic spells in my room to keep her from knowing I was practicing magic.

This was when I went to the Blue Moon magic shop for the first time. I wanted to get some magical incense to attract love. As I entered the shop, I saw a large glass counter and an enormous black cat. Behind the counter sat a woman in a lime green pantsuit with big black 1950s style hair with one solid white stripe down the middle like the Bride of Frankenstein.

That woman somehow looked right into my soul. "Hello, Houston," she said to me. "We've been waiting for you for a long time." I nearly jumped out of my skin. I have never forgotten that moment. I asked the woman how she knew my name. The chances of anyone being able to guess a name like Houston for a young black man must have been astronomical!

She then went on to tell me that I was born under a lucky star and that everything in life would come easy for me. She told me I had many talents and gifts. Still, I would have to overcome my natural ease of life to succeed and fulfill my destiny. I have never forgotten those words.

Days later, after partying all night with my sister and Tevin, I had run into an older guy I had sex with several times during high school. After the club, Tevin and I got in the car with him. We were all drunk and high. I gave Tevin the keys, and the guy and I made out in the back seat while Tevin drove us back to his apartment.

As I had to go home every night as part of my agreement with my parents, I asked Tevin if the guy could stay at his place, and I'd come pick him up in the morning. I figured it was fine since Tevin was straight. When I arrived in the morning, I found my so-called straight friend with his head down between the guy's legs. To say I was blown away would be an understatement. I wanted to be mad, but I couldn't stop laughing. To this day, he denies it ever happened. That was the beginning of the end of our friendship.

It was then that I began to recognize a pattern. From infancy to adulthood, I found myself in a continuous exhilaration stream that ultimately led to mistrust and disappointment. The wall that started at my feet was now firmly above my knees, and I was starting to stumble toward a downward spiral.

Interestingly enough, my taste in music changed as well. I still liked punk and dance music, but at this period, the music became heavier and darker. I was now a die-hard fan of bands like The Smiths, Cocteau Twins, Bauhaus, Love and Rockets, Cabaret Voltaire, Section 25, Ministry, Tones on Tail, Front 242, and the greatest of them all, Clan of Xymox. This was also when the Jewish lads from Brooklyn, better known as the Beastie Boys, made rap cool to white kids in every college from Miami to Seattle. It was the beginning of the end of rock music.

CHAPTER 28

DENVER "HIGHER" EDUCATION

My parents bought a beautiful new home on the west side of Lubbock. For the first time in my life, I felt like we were rich or at least upper-middle class. I was also thrilled to get accepted at Texas Tech University. I thought everything was somehow going to work out after all. I would get a degree and vindicate myself from all humiliation I had to endure in the Army. I was only 21. I was still young enough to get into the Olympics.

My whole attitude about life had taken a 180-degree turn. I no longer saw myself as the shy, confused boy hiding a dark secret. I was Houston, a fabulous queen who wasn't afraid to shout, "I'm gay" from the rooftops, from every barstool and nightclub dance floor, in every city or town I found myself in. Once my parents knew, I didn't give a damn anymore. I decided I wouldn't stay in the closet another minute.

I had developed a new sense of power and self-awareness that I'd never had before. I felt like I finally knew who I was and what I wanted. This new-found strength was fueled by my insatiable appetite for drugs, alcohol, and sex. I honestly don't think Lubbock was ready for me. I hadn't been back to Lubbock since we left in a hurry all those years ago. Honestly, I never thought I'd end up back there, but as fate would have it, there I was, and I took the whole town and Texas Tech by storm.

Before returning to Lubbock, I decided to visit my Aunt who lives in Colorado. I really couldn't tell you why I went since I barely knew her, and my only memories of her were unpleasant. For example, once she told my father that my sister and I were playing with guns, when in fact, we were trying to take a loaded gun away from the neighbor's kid. The kid had gotten into his father's gun cabinet and was running around the house, pointing a loaded rifle at everyone. My aunt's lie resulted in my sister and me taking a beating from my father. I didn't deserve that beating; I was doing the right thing, but my father didn't believe us. That was the first time I realized my father would take someone else's word over mine, even when I was telling the truth.

However, I made it to Denver and spent time really bonding with my aunt and her two sons. My aunt was stunning and had hypnotic green eyes that quite frankly gave me the creeps. But she was cool, and she liked to party. Her husband was a smooth cat playing in a well-known funk band. He was an impressive dude with a killer smile. Everything about him, down to his superfly hat said he was a player.

Strangely, I don't remember much of my time in Denver. However, later, Aunt's youngest son would thank me for being there during a difficult time between their mother and father. As he stood teary-eyed before me, I couldn't remember any of the things he was describing, but I played along anyway. He told me my aunt left them alone for days at a time so she could go fuck around and get high.

Nevertheless, everything was going really well on my little visit, which was a huge relief for me, especially since my mother begged me not to do anything to cause a stir while visiting Aunt Lane. She reminded me of how her sister loves to gossip, which meant what one sister knew, they all knew. Everything changed, however, on the last day before my flight home.

Earlier that day, Aunt Lane offered to give me a lift to the downtown area to go out and have some fun in Denver before I left to start school. Of course, this sounded great. To be honest, that was probably the real reason I decided to visit. This was my chance to go to a big city and find Mr. Right-Bear. I'd already made up my mind that my perfect bear was out there waiting for me on the dance floor at one of those big-city bars.

More importantly, I knew it would be a long time before I'd see a big city again. I was going to be spending the next four years living at home with my parents, a prospect I wasn't too thrilled about. Another contract I locked myself right into. This was also why I had no intentions of letting this golden opportunity pass me by.

Somewhere around 9:00 pm on my last evening, my aunt was dropping me off in downtown Denver. Before I got out of the car, she handed me a small piece of paper with her address and home telephone number. She instructed me to call her when I was ready to come home. I went from bar to bar, and to my surprise, I didn't hook up with anyone. I danced a lot and met a few fun fellows, but that was the long and short of it.

Before I knew it, the house lights at the last bar were flashing. The bartenders announced the last call for alcohol. Naturally, I ordered one last shot and made a short toast with whoever I was talking to at the bar. I told him I had to go, we hugged, and I went outside.

People were streaming out, some laughing and joking. I stood there watching all the mayhem. Then I suddenly remembered I had to call my aunt to get home. I reached into my pocket, looking for the piece of paper she had given me earlier and felt nothing. I checked my other pockets and again, nothing.

I mindlessly began to walk, wondering what I was going to do now. I stopped and turned around to look towards the bar, but the lights were off now, and the door was closed. The parking lot was virtually empty. Worst of all, there was no way to let anyone know where I was. It would be just a matter of hours before my aunt would call my mother, and everyone else would start looking for me.

As I stood there silently imploding, seemingly out of nowhere, a car pulled up next to me by the curb. The driver's window was down, and he leaned towards me, asking if I needed a ride. At that moment, I thought I was the luckiest guy on earth.

I looked at the man carefully. He was a big, bearish white man. Naturally, I trusted him. I will admit – I wanted a ride home, and I wanted *him* to give me that ride. The attraction to older chubby white males has directed most of my life choices, as you will see.

I started to explain my desperate situation and how grateful I am for the ride. He told me to get in the car, so I opened the door and continued to explain how I was not from Denver, and I was only visiting my aunt. Before I could finish explaining my situation, the guy said something that I didn't quite understand at first. "I only have $40," he said. I looked at him, feeling very confused. I told the weirdo I would give him gas money when we get to my aunt's house.

The guy just turned towards me, repeating the same thing he had said before, "All I have is 40 dollars!" I was starting to feel the "Danger, Will Robinson" vibe from this guy, but without really thinking, I replied, "If you want to give me $40, sure... I'll take it!"

Literally, not more than three seconds later, out of nowhere, police cars with blaring sirens, red and blue lights flashing from every direction surrounded the car. Next thing I know, a gang of police were shining flashlights in my face, violently dragging me from the car on the concrete pavement face first. My arms were forcefully, and very painfully I might add, pulled behind my back by the biggest, most butch lesbian dyke police officer I've ever seen on God's green earth.

I was told I was under arrest for male prostitution. I was shocked. I pleaded with the officers. I told them I didn't live there, that I was visiting from Texas. I begged those assholes not to arrest me. I begged them to please listen to me, but they just laughed in my face. They were 100 percent certain I was a hooker. I remember feeling shocked by the horrible things they were accusing me of doing. They said all kinds of nasty, racist, mean-spirited things to me and about me.

After the cops finished beating me and calling me a liar, I was taken downtown and booked for prostitution. In the city jail, they strip-searched me and placed me in a lineup with other prisoners. That was my first peek at jailhouse etiquette.

Two hardened-looking criminals flanked me. One was a creepy-looking black man that was truly hard on the eyes and the other one was a Mexican dude with a white wife beater and a bandana wrapped around his greasy hair. They both kept staring at me. I did my best to ignore them until the black guy started talking to me and rubbing his clearly visible semi-hard on. He kept looking me up and down in the worst kind of way. Then he said, "I can't wait till we get upstairs. I'm gonna tap that fat ass!"

I was freaking out because he wasn't the only one looking at me, but I tried to stay calm and just ignored the advances. Of course, I didn't want to get raped. By that time, AIDS was a guaranteed death sentence. So, when I reached the room where they separated people, I went to the guards and nurse and told them I was gay and couldn't be put in with the other prisoners. They moved me to another unit that was less scary but still frightening.

Let me tell you, jail sucks. It's so cold it's ridiculous. You have to wear these orange jumpsuits, and God only knows how many other men have worn them with their sweaty body parts. The food is complete and utter slop, and at night you can't sleep because they never turn the lights off. Worst of all, you have to use the toilet in the middle of your 8ft pod in front of your roommate. To some people, that might be considered homoerotic. To me, it's just disgusting and degrading on so many levels. No wonder criminals are so angry and pissed off all the time.

I spent the night in jail and didn't sleep a single minute. I knew my mother was going to be very unhappy. And like clockwork, my Aunt Lane did call my mom and let her know that I had never made it home that night. She had called the hospitals and the jailhouse, and that's how she found out I had been arrested for male prostitution. Of course she told everyone in the family, including my grandmother.

The cops let me go early that morning. All the charges against me had been dropped. They decided I was actually just lost. Go figure! But just like if someone accuses you of being a sex offender, and you are later found not guilty, there will still be those that doubt you.

I left Denver the very next day. We didn't talk about what happened ever again.

CHAPTER 29

TEXAS TECH

By 1986 Lubbock, Texas had grown from being a one-horse town to a full-fledged two-horse town, filled with in-the-closet country ass rednecks, ignorant black people, and enough non-English speaking wetbacks to populate half of Mexico. Lubbock had also become a serious party town with over 36,000 students. Texas Tech was the school you went to if you couldn't get accepted to the University of Texas or A&M. The town also had a small but thriving gay community, centered near the campus where there were several great gay bars, like Uncle Charlie's.

My first semester at Texas Tech was a blast. I felt like I was back on track, and I could see myself graduating with honors. I chose architecture as my major, and I wanted to minor in music. One thing the Army did do was give me confidence. Before I first stepped on campus, I had determined that I was going to be openly gay. I was trained in martial arts and wasn't afraid to fight anyone. I was ex-military, and I'd been fighting older men from the time I was a teenager. Well, in this case, I was actually the older man. I was about to turn 21 that year, and everyone thought I was the coolest guy on campus.

I was always dressed in black. I wore makeup, I permed my hair straight and let it grow really long on the top so that it covered my face, and I kept it short on the sides. I wore earrings in both ears and always wore a pair of black leather punk rock boots, crosses around my neck, and leather bracelets. I even wore a skirt from time to time.

I thought I wanted to be in a frat. There were a lot of frat houses, and they were all the same in principle. Except for the one or two all-black fraternities and one or two frats like Sigma Chi (SX) that were open to all, 99.9 % of the frats were lily-white. In those days, Sigma Chi (SX) was where all the losers and lower-middle-class kids ended up. Other than that, it was pretty cool, and I was actually proud to be accepted. I pledged for about 3 or 4 weeks before I thought I'd rather keep my money. I had figured out I could still go to all the frat parties without being a pledge.

Not too long after, I quit the frat. I had stopped going to classes altogether. To be honest, I had even stopped going to campus. More and more, I was staying out all night partying into the next day, and many times I didn't go home for several days, which caused my parents to take away my car. I responded by moving out.

I got the idea to move out from an older Mexican man named Mr. Fernando that I'd met one night. In the 1980s, Texas's entire state was an interconnected ring of gay and straight XXX bookstores. These bookstores all had a back area with "private booths" that customers could go into and watch XXX movies. Inside the booths, you would find a large hole in the wall.

I can't count the number of married men who frequented these places daily. You could set your watch by their arrival; at noon, the place would be full of straight and married guys. The second rush was right after work from 5 to 8 pm. Then finally, the late-night pervs would show up between 12-2 am. I'd often think about how their wives didn't know and what they would do if they did.

It was in one of those sleazy XXX bookstores that I met Mr. Fernando. After our rendezvous, he took me to lunch, and we hooked up a few times. I mentioned to him one time as we were lying in bed that I wanted to move out of my parents' house. He told me that he had a place I could stay. It was a great offer, so I moved in.

Not even a week went by, and he was coming over every second of the day, wanting me to give him sexual favors. I remember how dirty I felt.

He made me feel like he had bought me like a slave or a prostitute. That was my first lesson in the realities of being gay. Finally, I said something horrible and left.

I couldn't go back to my parents. That was definitely out of the question. Especially since by doing so I would have admitted they were right, and I would be forced back under their anti-gay Christian rule. So, I went to the university dorm and stayed with my friend Kent for a week or so until I found a place with two other guys I'd met partying at the underground punk club called Lizard Lounge.

One of my roommates was my little Asian buddy, Thai. He showed me how to make proper ramen noodles, and he had the best taste in music of anyone I've ever met. My other roommate was a white guy named Mike. Mike was this crazy dude that literally thought he was the coolest guy on earth. I hated his taste in music, but he was a likable guy.

Everybody knew Mike, and he knew everybody. This was because Mike was by far the biggest drug dealer on campus. I don't think he often went to class, instead, he paid people to do his homework and take tests. Not long after moving in together, Mike sat us down and offered to let us in on his business. This is how we also started selling drugs.

As Mike didn't go to the gay bars, it was a virgin territory to exploit, and I exploited it to the fullest. I never considered the consequences of being caught selling all those drugs, and I'd all but forgotten about getting my degree. I was in a daze and completely lost.

I learned the power of cocaine and ecstasy. I found myself many times that year in one situation after another with straight guys trading sex with me for cocaine. Back then, if I found a guy attractive, and he didn't have the money to pay me, I'd offer him an alternative way to pay me. I never had one guy say no to me. The moral of the story for me was simple: Cocaine makes even a straight man temporarily gay.

Something else was happening around that time that would have a profound effect on my psyche. My obsession with a little-known band from Manchester, England called The Smiths was growing stronger by the day. The music of The Smiths would become the soundtrack of my life for many years to come and the lens that I would see the world through from one heartache to another.

Punk and new wave had transmuted into two different schools of thought in 1986. On one end of the spectrum, groups like Xymox, Front 242, and Skinny Punny formed the epicenter of the new genre called dark industrial. On the other end of the stick, you had groups like The Smiths, The Housemartins, and Gene Loves Jezebel that sang songs about love and sexuality in a way that had never been done before.

Groups like Bronski Beat had opened the floodgates for homoerotic anthems. Still, The Smiths were definitely the MVPs of every little gay man from London to Omaha. At Texas Tech, The Smiths were the kings of the displaced and disaffected youth. You couldn't go to frat parties without hearing The Smiths played at least ten times a night. Even the straight boys and girls sang along with Morrissey's clever and provocative lyrics as if they were the gospel. The greatest and the most popular song was "How Soon Is Now?" This epic song is still just as relevant and powerful as it was back then.

For months I spent my time around Texas Tech's sprawling campus, pretending to be a serious student, selling and doing more drugs than the law allowed and meeting men. But none of those guys caught my attention until I met Rob. He was a student administrator and at least a good 10-15 years older than me. He was my first college love.

We met at the local gay bar during a wild night out with my usual group of friends. We were definitely the "it" crowd around the local bar scene mainly because I was a drug dealer and lived with the most popular drug dealer on campus. At that point I was the only openly gay person that I knew at Texas Tech.

We had taken several ecstasy pills. I personally believe ecstasy is the single biggest reason we have so many bisexual people today. It certainly made many students in 1986, gay or straight, turn bisexual, at least while rolling. One of my most intense drug/sex-related experience also came the night I met Rob. I was lost in a heavy French-kissing session with a girl I didn't really know. We looked at each other and asked, "What was that all about?" It was incredibly awkward because her boyfriend was sitting next to her and didn't seem to mind. That was when I noticed Rob. He looked over at me, and we started talking and chatting about the music. Ten minutes later, he asked me if I wanted to get out of there. Of course, I did.

We spent that night together having extasy-induced passionate sex for seven hours as we listened to Clan of Xymox over and over on his stereo cassette player until the tape broke from rewinding it too much. I instantly fell in love. For most of my adult life, I found myself quickly and naively attaching to any man that showed the slightest interest in me. I was starved for love and intimacy, and the only way I felt loved was when a certain type of man desired me. It's impossible to understand the impact molestation had on my life and the unwanted problems it created for me.

I also had a strong desire to get love and attention from my father and mother. I grew up under a system of punishment and reward where there was absolutely no middle ground. Now don't get me wrong, I know that my parents loved me, but we rarely spoke about any feelings or emotions. A quote from the Bible answered everything, and that was the end of that every discussion. We rarely hugged or kissed like other families. I imagine one could say I was starving for love emotionally and physically, and if anyone showed me the slightest attention, I would jump into a relationship with both feet time and time again.

CHAPTER 30

THERE IS A LIGHT

In less than one year, I had pretty much dropped out of college. I wasn't going to class or even pretending that I was a student anymore. I had essentially become a full-time partier and part-time drug dealer.

The house we lived in was just off campus and a few blocks away from the bars and the adult bookstores. It was a pretty cool place as far as houses go, and we were a pretty cool set of roommates as far as roommates go. We had the carefree, pretty, rich white womanizer, the super cool rich Asian kid that played the best music, and the openly gay, black, goth kid. Being openly gay made me a target for closeted gay boys and even straight men.

I often received late-night phone calls from people asking me if I wanted to "have a couple of beers."

Then something unexpected happened. One night after partying and dancing and selling drugs in the gay bars, I decided to stop at the adult bookstore just a few blocks down the road from my house. I was really high and definitely on a mission.

The bookstores are all pretty much the same no matter what town, city, state, or country you are in. The layout is generally set with a creepy-looking guy or sometimes a rocker chick behind the counter. The walls are covered from floor to ceiling with XXX-rated DVDs, sex toys, and porno magazines, gay and straight. Near the back (or sometimes near the front), a doorway leads to a maze of private booths where guys sit or stand and put tokens into a machine to relieve themselves watching porn on the monitors.

Somehow, I always managed to overlook how filthy these places really were and how bad they really smelled. How many dirty older men had relieved themselves in there just in the last 30 minutes? I mean, sure, they had janitors who cleaned up the mess. However, you have to admit it's pretty unsanitary by anyone's standards.

That night I needed satisfaction. As I was wandering past the video booths looking for an open door, I came across a guy leaning against the wall. He was a very tall, blond-haired, blue-eyed bearish white man. He wasn't the cutest guy, but as our eyes met, he reminded me of the chubby babysitter. He looked at me like I was someone special. He was older than me, that was obvious, and honestly, that was the first thing I liked about him.

I smiled at him, and he smiled back. We started talking, and we instantly connected. He told me his name was Ben. He made me feel safe and relaxed. He had a warm and affectionate way about him, and he was calm and confident. He was 18 years older than me, and his sign was Cancer like my father. According to astrology, we were a good match. Not a perfect match but doable.

We talked and maybe even messed around in the bookstore video room. We decided to leave, and Ben drove us out to his house in a one-traffic-light town just outside of the Lubbock city limits. We spent the night in his backyard, lying on the grass staring at the stars. We must have been a sight to behold, lying there next to each other. Ben was 6'3" and 250lbs. I was 5'8" and maybe a buck fifty soaking wet in those days.

Within days of our chance meeting at the bookstore, we were dating. I don't remember many other times in my life that I was as happy as I was with Ben. Things went from me just coming over to hang out and staying the night to be virtually living with him in a matter of weeks. It turned out that Ben was the mayor of the little town, and he was in the closet. We told people I was a student, and Ben was renting me a room. This was my first experience in a real relationship, and for the second time, I thought I had found true love. I started to call Ben's house my home. We lived like a couple, just like I remembered watching on TV growing up. My dreams had come true.

Even though I was 21 years old, I still had the kind of parents that wanted to know where and with whom I was spending all my time. So, I finally got the courage to tell them that I had moved in with a man and that we were a couple. I expected my parents to be angry and double down on their condemnation of my homosexual lifestyle, but to my surprise, they agreed to meet him.

I was excited for my parents to meet Ben, and plans were made for dinner the following Saturday night. I don't know if you are old enough to remember the classic film, *Guess Who's Coming to Dinner*, but that was what it was like. I was so nervous, but Ben was relaxed, cool, calm, and collected like always. There are no words to describe the look on my parents' faces when they answered the door and saw me standing there with this "old" man. They literally looked like they both had seen a ghost. Ben just smiled, extended his hand, and said hello. My father and mother stood frozen for a good 30 seconds before regaining their usual Southern decorum.

The first thing my mother asked was, "So... Mr. Ben, how old are you?" I thought my mother was going to choke when Ben replied. I have to admit

I, too, felt awkward hearing Ben's age out loud in front of my parents. That was the first time I thought that Ben was the same age as my mother.

My parents were clearly uncomfortable, although they did their best to be polite and gracious. I remember my mother did what she had so often done with my friends: she asked Ben if he knew the Lord Jesus Christ as his personal Lord and Savior.

After the dinner party, Ben and I drove back to his place. We sang The Smiths songs all the way home. Our favorite song was "There is a Light That Never Goes Out." It was our song and is still one of my favorites.

Ben loved music with the same passion and devotion as me, and best of all, he loved my music, which endeared him to me more than anyone before or since. Ben also exposed me to a new world of 60s and 70s rock that I would eventually grow to love just as much as my goth and punk rock music.

One day Ben got a call from someone who had just become a candidate for a high-level elected state official. As Ben came out of his study and sat down next to me in the living room, I could tell he was very excited. He told me that he had just been asked to be the manager for a big campaign. I said, "That's great, Ben." I was really happy for him.

He told me he would have to move to Austin, and before I could say anything, he asked me if I wanted to go with him. I said, "But what about school? What about my parents?" Ben assured me, as he so often did,

175

that everything would be fine. He told me I could simply enroll at Austin Community College, fix my grades, and then transfer to the University of Texas, which at the time sounded like the perfect plan. Had I followed his simple plan, I'd probably be a Professor of History today. But life and destiny would take me in a completely different direction.

You see, music was the driving force in my life. My favorite bands beckoned me to join them in the Rock & Roll Hall of Fame. Moving to the live music capital of the world, for a person like me, was like arriving in Mecca after a pilgrimage of a thousand miles with no shoes. Austin was, and still is, one of the centers of American music. There are more bands and artists in Austin per capita than any other place in America. LA had its hard rock, glam rock, and hip hop. Nashville had the country, and New York was the land of indie rock, punk, and hip hop. But Austin had everything, rock, punk, hip hop, jazz, blues, country, and even rockabilly.

Of course, I agreed to move with Ben. We packed up his house, and the movers came to relocate us to Austin. It was a beautiful city. The rolling hills and the tree-lined roads were in stark contrast to Lubbock's flat plains and dusty roads. In Austin, there were hipsters and rockers, blues singers and jazz musicians, metalheads, dreadlocked Rastas, cowboys, and thousands of students, and everyone got along. And there were gay bars… lots and lots of gay bars.

My life evolved overnight. I was suddenly affluent by association. Ben was making more money than anyone I knew at the time. I would find out over the years that Ben was very good with money. He owned rental properties and had perfect credit and more credit cards than anyone I have ever known. We never talked about money or finance, and I don't think I ever asked him to buy me anything. Most of the time, he would offer or surprise me with something he knew I liked.

I never looked at money as a motivation for a relationship, either then or now. That, too, is more than likely due to my early molestation. To me, love was sex and security. I wanted to feel safe. Money has never been able to give me that feeling.

Ben rented us an upscale condo just across the bridge on 1st Street. At first, I stayed at home. I spent my days listening to records and smoking weed, drinking vodka tonics, and binge eating waiting for Ben to get home. I would make dinner, and we would eat and go to bed. Not that I had it bad, but I became unhappy and started drinking more.

Soon, the calls from my mother began telling me that I was living in sin, and she started repeating her mantra, "Nothing is ever going to go right for you, son, until you get right with the Lord." This went on for some time, and that's when I stopped answering the phone. Ben would often tell my parents that I wasn't in, and he'd have me call them back.

Meanwhile, I wanted to start a band, and to do that, I needed a job to buy instruments. This also meant I'd hold off on school for a while. I told Ben what I wanted to do, and he thought it was a great idea. Ben was always supportive of me as an artist.

Ben recommended I apply with the State. To any normal person, getting a great job working in the heart of Texas politics would have been enough. But I wasn't a normal guy. I had my mind fixed on one thing, and that was becoming a rock star. You see, I hadn't forgotten about my friend Tevin and how he and his band snubbed me. I was going to show them all that I was the real star. I put an ad in the *Austin Chronicle* looking for musicians who were influenced by The Cure, Love and Rockets, Bauhaus, Ministry, The Smith, and Siouxsie and the Banshees.

I also applied for and got a job as a runner for the representatives at the state Capitol. I did use Ben as a reference, but somehow, I still wanted to believe I got the job independently. Working at the Capitol was a major boost to my self-esteem. Also, it was one of the easiest jobs I ever had. Basically, they paid me to do nothing.

I was one of about ten other runners that worked for the House of Representatives. The runners' room was in the basement, next to the toilets that we often used to snort cocaine and sip vodka from the bottle stashed in a book bag. Most of the runners were political science majors, the offspring of a wealthy Texas family or business associates of a Congressman. Our room reminded me of the after-school detention scene from *The Breakfast Club*. There were moments of excitement, but I spent most of those six months making copies, dropping off mail and packages, and doing cocaine with spoiled, rich white kids.

CHAPTER 31

WELL, HOWDY Y'ALL,
WELCOME TO AUSTIN

I didn't work in the Capitol for very long. That entry-level job opened the door for me to get a job at the Texas State Commission. It just so happened that Ben and his boss were the head honchos. I was a clerk in the Records Department, a few floors below Ben and his boss's top-floor office. My boss was a middle-aged Hispanic woman. She was a sharp cookie, and she ran a tight ship. I think she genuinely liked me, but she was definitely afraid of me. I was treated with kid gloves, and I got away with murder when it came to bending the rules.

It all started when one morning my floor supervisor saw Ben and me getting out of the car together. The sighting sparked a wildfire of rumors and speculation in my department about Ben and me. The next day my boss called me into her office. I had expected I would be written up for being out at lunch break. I sat down and was fully prepared to explain why I was late. Still, before I could speak, my boss began to lay out this tale of cloak and dagger that took me completely by surprise.

As it turned out, she and the other supervisors and my colleagues, 95% of which were women, had concluded that I was a spy for the Director's office, and I was there to report to the commissioner about their performance. I couldn't believe how naive my boss was to not even consider the possibility of Ben and I being lovers.

As I sat there listening to my boss plead with me to let her keep her job, it took everything within me not to laugh. After she finished, I assured her I wasn't a spy and that Ben and I were just good friends. I don't think she believed me, but that was the last time I was reprimanded for being late.

I had no idea about Texas politics or just how important Ben and his campaign was. I knew the candidate he was working for was running for the top job in Texas politics, but that was pretty much all I knew or even wanted to know. I was falling in love with Ben and Austin, so I didn't care if he was a plumber or the president of the United States. A dream had come true, not just for me, but I believe for Ben as well. I had found true love, and I thought it would last forever.

I had laid off the partying and focused all my attention on Ben and our happiness. We did everything together. He was becoming my best friend, and he was a pretty good cook. Our home was elegant and filled with expensive antiques. Although our condo was quite lovely at 900 square feet, it was too small for us, and this issue soon became critical. Something had to be done. I felt like a sardine trapped inside the condo day in and day out.

One day Ben and I were having dinner when the phone rang, which was rare because the only person who called for me was my mom. But on this occasion, it was a guy named Dirk Landis. Dirk had read my ad in the *Austin Chronicle*, and he wanted to know if I was still looking for a musician. Dirk was a ball of fire, and I just gravitated to his energy. We decided to meet over the weekend.

Dirk was a freshman at UT, and he had the worst-looking acne. But he could play the drums and guitar, and we liked the same music. A band was born. I told him the band's name was Andrew and that I took the name from a villainous *Star Trek* character named Landru. Some days later, we turned the spare room in our two-bedroom apartment into a recording studio /rehearsal space. How in the world Ben and my neighbors put up with all that racket, I don't know, but I'm happy they did.

A couple of weeks later, Ben asked me to take a ride out to South Austin. After driving for about 30 minutes, we arrived at an undeveloped neighborhood filled with dirt-covered empty lots. We pulled up to one of them, and Ben told me we were building a house from the ground up to have everything just the way we wanted. I was blown away. Nine months later, we moved into the most beautiful two-story brick home.

The house was set at the end of a cul-de-sac on one acre of woodland filled with squirrels, all types of birds, and wild deer. It had four big bedrooms. One of the rooms was my recording and practice studio, and there were two nicely appointed guest rooms for family and friends.

"My room" was fully furnished and decorated to my taste, with posters of my favorite bands hung on the walls. We even put in soundproofing. As Ben was deep in the closet, the entire room, down to the clothes in the wardrobe and the toothbrush in the bathroom, was made to look like I slept in there – a ruse for Ben's family members, friends, or co-workers who came to visit.

He often took me to political dinners and cocktail parties, where I stood out like a sore thumb. I was always answering questions about my relationship with Ben and my political affiliations.

CHAPTER 32

DEMONS OF ROCK

Life was going along perfectly. One could say I had it all. All I had to do was sit back and relax, and Ben and I could have been the happiest couple in the world. But I wanted more. I wanted to be a star.

Slowly, my full attention turned to music and the band. Andrew was my brainchild, it was my band, and I knew who and what I wanted it to be. At work I spent hours writing songs and poems hidden between rows and rows of tall metal file cabinets pretending to file records. I constantly wrote on scraps of paper and even on my hand. I had notebook after notebook of songs and poetry in every drawer in the house.

I had begun writing in college at Texas Tech. English was my favorite class at that time and the only one I actually attended more than twice. I had a brilliant professor who knew how to get the best out of me. One of my assignments was to write a book of poetry. After we had turned in our body of work at the end of the semester, we would receive a grade and her personal comments.

I received a "B." Later I asked my professor why she did not give me an "A" for my work. She replied, "Your writing is wonderful, and you have a gift for words. However, if nobody can understand the meaning behind those beautiful words, the work has no value to anyone but you." She went on to explain the importance of writing for an audience. I have never forgotten that lesson.

The band's first gig was a disaster. It was at a place called Black Cat Lounge right at the top of 6th Street. The legendary place was known worldwide for its great live blues, jazz, and rock acts. The place had the look of a biker bar and had the clientele to match.

I had spent the previous year hanging out at the Black Cat buying drinks and throwing money around, which eventually got the attention of the now-deceased owner, Paul. We got to know each other, and I could tell he genuinely liked me. One night I got the courage to ask him if my band could play a gig at his bar. Boy, was I surprised when he said, "Sure, why not?" He never asked to hear a demo. He just gave me a date for the following month.

I'd never been so excited. Finally, my band had its first gig, and as far as I was concerned, rock stardom was just around the corner. We practiced every day right up until the day of the gig. Ben was even more excited than me. He told all his friends, and he even surprised me and had band T-shirts made for all of us.

On the night of the gig, I was so nervous and anxious I must have had at least 10 shots of vodka. I was already intoxicated by the time we got on stage. The place was packed with as many people as Black Cat could hold. Ben was there in the back with his Andrew T-shirt on, having a cocktail with a few of his friends.

We were the opening act. We plugged in our amps, and we started to play our set. The rest is a blur. The only thing I remember about that night was walking over to the bar after the set to ask Paul how we did. I will never forget the look of horror on his face. He said we were the worst band he'd ever seen. Then he politely asked me never to play at his bar again. Then he poured me another shot, and we both laughed.

I took Paul's words to heart, and the very next day, I fired our drummer and Kirk, and I doubled our efforts. We went through five drummers before I got a call from my old pal Tevin. He was down on his luck, working at a restaurant. His band had broken up, and I could sense he was looking for a change. I suggested he join my band. After all, we needed a drummer, and Tevin was definitely a kick-ass drummer. So, I offered to buy him a ticket to Austin, and he moved in with me and Ben in the big house in the hills of Austin.

The band's sound and look transformed. Suddenly we went from the joke of 6th Street to playing gigs every weekend at the best alternative rock clubs in the city. I remember the first time a fan asked me for my autograph after a show at the now-defunct Cannibal Club. I was blown away. I wanted more of that feeling.

Andrew became my all-consuming passion. I was clearly the leader of the band. Most of the gear belonged to me, and I wrote all the songs and all the music. I soon began to cast magical spells and call on spiritual beings to help us become rock gods. I even put curses on rival bands I didn't like or felt threatened by. One evening Dirk, Tevin, and I went to see U2. After the show, we stood outside the stadium and performed an impromptu dark spell to make Andrew come to life whenever the three of us gathered to play music.

Sadly, Andrew turned out to be a monster, and the worst part was that we started to believe we were rock gods. We all started partying out of control, as opportunity after opportunity came to us. The more popular we became, the more people just started hanging around. Suddenly, strangers were my best buddies. When you're the lead singer of the band, everybody wants to be your friend, and everybody knew the way to be my best friend was to give me drugs, lots of drugs.

At the time, vodka, acid, and weed were my drugs of choice, and I indulged every chance I got. And most importantly, I didn't give a shit about anyone but me. We each had our own followers, but as the lead singer, I was always the center of attention. Unfortunately, I hardly remember any of it because 95% of the time I was either high or drunk or some combination of the two.

But the band rocked, and that's all that mattered in those days. You see, at some point, we realized that the more outrageous and more fucked up we were, the more people liked us. So, we got fucked up every night, we got on stage, and we rocked! We were booked two, three, sometimes four nights a week. We performed on TV and in the best places in town.

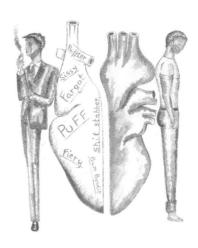

CHAPTER 33

IT'S JUST POLITICS

The first years in Austin went by fast, and my band was kicking ass! My home life was perfect too. I was totally devoted to Ben even though there were a few incidents of coke and alcohol-induced indiscretions, which left me feeling ashamed and undeserving of his love. Nevertheless, I knew I loved him, and overall, I was happy.

It felt like we were a married couple, and I saw myself spending the rest of my life with him. Ben seemed happy too. He was my biggest fan and came to every gig. He was really proud of me. Everyone knew he was my boyfriend. His campaign work was going great, he was busy doing his thing, and I was proud of him too.

But as cliché as this might sound, the unthinkable happened. I came home one night after practice. I felt great and super excited because the band had a show coming up that weekend. When I walked into the living room, I saw Ben sitting in his favorite chair. He was smoking a cigarette, which was something I'd only seen him do maybe once before. He looked white as a sheet.

I stood there looking at him and asked him what was wrong. He told me to sit down. With tears running down his face, he told me he had been on the phone for most of the evening talking to the candidate whose campaign he was running. The candidate told Ben he had received a call from the opposing campaign team stating that they had known about his campaign manager and his young gay black lover.

I didn't say anything. I walked into the kitchen and made a drink. When I walked back into the living room, Ben told me that the candidate said he had not believed the rumor and that he knew I was just a friend of the family. But to avoid any more "misunderstandings," I had to move out.

I can't put my feelings and emotions into words. My ears went deaf, and he faded out as he told me I'd only have to be gone for a few months. I never said a word. I just turned around, went to the bedroom, and cried. I understood how important his career was to him, and running a major campaign was his dream, but deep down, I hoped he would tell me our love was more important than public opinion. But that never happened.

A few days later, the band helped me move out to an apartment Ben had rented for 3 months in advance near 6th Street. I should have been happy, but inside I was exploding like a nuclear bomb. That was the first time in my life I knew what it was like to have a broken heart. I cried all night in that beautiful apartment, listening to the haunting music of the Cocteau Twins. I cried until I could not cry anymore and finally fell asleep.

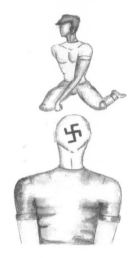

CHAPTER 34

LEARNING TO HATE

At first, Ben came to see me every day. We would meet for lunch a couple of times a week, then once a week, he dropped by for sex. After some weeks I decided to go out to the house and see him. After all, I still had keys to the house.

When I got to the house, everything felt different. Ben spoke to me very formally. There was an older guy there, who had his feet up on the coffee table and appeared to be right at home. Ben introduced me as a friend from back in Lubbock and told me the guy was going to begin renting a room.

That night I decided that the relationship was over. I started using more drugs than ever. I started frequenting the gay bars, the bookstores, the parks, and the leather bars. I became unbearable to my friends and my own band.

A few weeks later, after rehearsals, we decided to go to Liberty Lunch, a spot all the bigger alternative bands like Sonic Youth, Fishbone, or Wu-Tang Clan would perform. GWAR was playing, so we dropped acid and headed to the show. I pulled up front and let Tevin and Dirk out while I drove around to the side to park. Then I walked back towards the building's side to meet Tevin and Dirk, who were waiting for me out front. We had a rule: we always stayed together in a club. We wanted to always look like a band.

As I came around the building, I saw my old friend Sean leaning against the wall standing next to a skinhead punk girl. I'd been around skinheads before, and I'd never had an issue with them. As I passed them, I said, "Hello, Sean, what's up?" He was acting like he didn't know me. So, I stopped and stood in front of him, thinking maybe he didn't see my face, and I said hello again, but this time he simply looked down at the ground and said nothing. I spoke to him again, "Sean, it's Houston from Lubbock."

Before I could say another word, the girl standing next to him stepped forward and said, "Get lost, you fucking nigger!" I couldn't believe what I was hearing. I looked at Sean and said, "Sean, bro, what is going on?" The girl gave me a glaring stare of defiance and said, "Look, nigger, you better get the fuck out of here, or my boyfriend is going to kick your fucking nigger ass!"

I stood there, frozen by rage and confusion. I had even played a gig with Sean's band, the Squat Thrust, in Lubbock when we were students at Texas Tech. Why was he so weird now? Who was this girl? For the life of me, I couldn't get my head around what I was witnessing. I asked him one last time what was going on.

Sean just looked away like he didn't know me. Once again, the girl said, "Get the fuck out of here, or my boyfriend is going to kick your fucking nigger ass!" I snapped and yelled, "Fuck you and your fucking boyfriend..." But before I could utter another word, I had a fist as big as my head smash into my cheeks from out of nowhere. I remember feeling my knees buckle underneath me like rubber noodles. I'd felt that kind of blow before, thanks to years of fighting in the ring. For the average guy it would have been a knockout punch, but I wasn't your average guy.

In seconds I was struck by another massive blow to the right side of my head that sent me spinning around in slow motion, like a replay of a heavyweight knockout punch. Luckily for me, all my years of martial arts training took over. I instantly recovered my balance as I kept myself from spinning to the ground before he could strike me again. Without thinking, I quickly picked up a Heineken bottle I spotted on the ground next to my feet.

The beast lunged at me again, but this time I was ready, I was fast, and I smashed the bottle in his face. Blood poured out, covering his face and his eyes, causing him to stop in his tracks. The next thing I knew, he was shouting, "Get my gun, I'm going to kill this nigger."

Fortunately, the cavalry arrived just in time. Apparently, my friends, who were waiting for me in front of the bar, came looking for me. About five or six of them saw what was happening and rushed over. One of my friends shouted, "Get out, Houston, get out of here!" That's when I saw the skinhead pointing a gun in my direction. I immediately started running. I ran some twenty blocks to The Ritz and banged on the door for the owner to let me in. I spent the rest of the night in sheer terror.

Later that night, I found out my attacker was a leader of the Dallas chapter of the skinheads named John Dagger. The police wanted him for stabbings and other assaults. I was beyond freaked out; I was traumatized. For weeks I was afraid to leave my apartment because I'd been told the skinheads were looking for me.

Finally, I decided to leave town and go to Dallas for a couple of months. At some point, I got a call from Dirk telling me that John Dagger had been arrested for murder. I returned to Austin, but I would never be the same again. I hated white people, and I wanted revenge.

I wrote a song about my experience called "Crushed." The lyrics were straightforward and right to the point.

"White man

Pay for your crimes

For all my people

Standing in the lines.

For all my perceptions

You don't realize

And all your deceptions.

You don't recognize

White man

Can't you see

Oh, why can't you see me."

This, however, deepened the rift that was growing in the band into a gagging chasm. Dirk, being white, hated the song and argued I was a racist. He didn't want to play the song, but Tevin, being black, convinced him it was racist *not* to play it. Ironically enough, that song became one of our most popular songs at our live shows.

Despite all the attention we were getting from the Austin music scene, the band was nearing its final curtain call. Heck, we were even approached by Mega Force Records and Wax Tracks and had a loyal following and a manager. Still, by that time, we really all hated each other. It was clear Andrew was falling apart, and everyone could see it.

I lashed out at everyone and everything. We argued more and more about things like what songs to play and who should sing what songs and what parts sucked, and which parts didn't suck. But, in the end, I always got my way, which made Dirk and Tevin hate me even more. It was around this time that I met Kevin.

CHAPTER 35

BEAUTY & THE BEAST

I'd actually met Kevin the year before while partying after a gig at a popular gay nightspot called The Boathouse. The Boathouse was an amazing place with the best DJs in town, and more importantly, the best drinks specials in Austin. Everyone in the city, gay or straight, knew about the famous Wednesday night 10-cent drinks specials. The place was owned by a former professional football player, who was in the closet. Back then half the gay men I knew were all still in the closet. It was also the time we all started hearing about a new disease called AIDS.

The place was always packed wall to wall. It was upstairs in the lounge where I first met Kevin. I had just come from playing a show on 6th Street, and I walked over to say hi to him. He looked at the way I was dressed and started laughing at me. He said I looked like a freak. I probably did look like a freak with my permed long straight hair, black lipstick, black nail polish, and all-black goth gear. Naturally, I told him to fuck off.

But when I saw him again, I was a different person. After the skinhead attack, I had a bad acid trip that resulted in me standing in front of a mirror crying my eyes out, taking a pair of dull scissors, and cutting my long blue-black hair off completely. I guess you could say I looked normal.

Kevin was sitting on the barstool next to me. I leaned over and asked, "Do you remember me?" He laughed and said, "Yeah, you're the freak from The Boathouse." We both laughed, and he said, "You look good." We talked some more, then he invited me to come to see him DJ at a place called Uncle Charlie's. I said, "Sure, why not?" After all, I had not heard from Ben for a couple of months, and I figured we were pretty much over.

Before I knew it, my world changed again overnight. After just one night I was madly in lust with Kevin's physical attributes. I knew I wasn't in love with him. He was the complete opposite of Ben. He was DJ at a gay bar, he was uneducated and lived in an apartment with no furniture except a mattress on the floor, a few porn magazines, and some rather large sex toys. He was 6'3" with curly black hair and a Texas-size personality that I found attractive. He was a very well-endowed, stocky white man close to 300 lbs. He was in much better shape than Ben, and he was only two years older than me. He was a wild-eyed Texas country boy that had a libido to match my own.

Within a week, Kevin asked me to move in with him, mainly because he didn't like Tevin. So, I packed up and moved out of the house that I rented with Tevin after the lease on the apartment Ben had rented for me had run out. I was sick of the band at that point, and I needed some space. Tevin never forgave me for moving out on him. He would later blame me for all his misfortunes and accuse me of abandoning him.

At first, things were great with Kevin and me. I used my excellent credit score I had established to furnish his apartment fully. I found myself hanging out at the gay bar where he worked 5-6 nights a week. I started to make friends with his friends and left my old friends behind. I was the belle of the ball, and everyone wanted to be my friend.

The thing about working in gay bars is everyone from the owners down to the janitor did coke. I mean everyone. Drug dealers were treated like celebrities. The only person more popular than the drug dealers was the DJ. As my boyfriend was the DJ at the most popular bar in town, everyone gave him coke. He rarely paid for it, and at first, I didn't have to either. This was the start of my years of addiction to cocaine. It all seemed like harmless fun at first. I mean, everyone was doing it, and we were just having a good time, right? But my good time would quickly turn into a horrible nightmare.

Two weeks after moving in with Tevin, my band broke up for good. The week before, Dirk had said he wanted out of the band. His girlfriend, who was a rep for Sony records, had convinced him that we were holding him back and that he was the band's real talent. So, in desperation to keep the band together, I told Dirk that if he stayed, he could have my guitar and my amp he had been using all this time since he was always broke and couldn't afford his own gig.

The next week Tevin and I were left standing in front of Club Marco Caribbean before our gig, wondering where the hell Dirk was. He showed up about 10 minutes before we were supposed to go on. I thought I was going to lose my mind. My head felt like it was going to explode; that was probably the angriest I've been in my adult life at another human being.

I expected him to jump out of his car, apologizing and grabbing his gear as fast as he could. Instead, he rolled down the window of his rusted red truck and shouted, "Guys, I quit!" Then he drove off. And that was that. Years of practice, thousands of dollars, and more headaches than the average man could stand… all for nothing. The band was done and dusted.

The downward spiral continued as things in my relationship and personal life began to unwind in every direction. Kevin was a lovable giant 99% of the time. I dare say he was the most popular gay man in Austin. But I soon discovered that he had a dark side, and you could always find it at the bottom of an empty bottle of Southern Comfort.

There was something almost supernatural that would happen whenever he drank. He was literally Jekyll and Hyde. Unfortunately for me, I became his favorite victim. I remember the first time he hit me after calling me a nigger in front of everyone at the bar. The Southern Comfort was working full force that night, and his right hook made my knees give way.

The violence had come to the level: we were threatening each other with broom handles, ironing boards, and knives. It was getting worse with each passing day. Our relationship became a living nightmare. Every morning I woke to wonder which Kevin I would have to deal with that day. Cocaine, cigarettes, and getting high replaced all my previous ambitions. I'd forgotten about everything that was once important to me.

All my so-called friends had abandoned me. After Fred opened his big mouth, I had become a pariah and told everyone I knew that I was shooting up, including Kevin, who promptly kicked me out. I lived on the streets for about a week until I begged him to let me back in the apartment. We told each other that we loved each other, and it was the drugs that were tearing us apart, so we decided to give our relationship one more try.

Unfortunately, the abuse continued for the next three years, ultimately ending with Kevin spending a few days in jail for assault. Only then did I have the willpower to finally leave him. I had to escape, or I knew I wasn't going to make it. Something bad was going to happen to me, and I could feel it getting closer every day.

I know you're asking yourselves why I did not leave sooner. The answer now seems obvious. It was sex. The sex between Kevin and I was, and probably still is, the best sex I've ever had in my 50-plus years of walking this earth. Somehow, every time I tried to leave after one of our epic knock-down battles, Kevin would sober up the next day and become the sweetest, kindest, most lovely guy in the world, and the make-up sex always made me unpack my bags and stay with him. It wasn't love, that's for sure. I think I pretty much hated Kevin by then.

I knew in my heart that my life was in danger; not only from my alcoholic, violent boyfriend, but also from the dangerous amounts of drugs I was injecting into my once virgin arms. I was also constantly hiding from a drug dealer I had ripped off by doing all the drugs he fronted me. I knew it was time to leave.

Kevin worked at the bar seven days a week. He left the house every day at the same time and usually did not come back home until 4 or 5 am. On the day of my escape, I waited until Kevin left for work and called a friend I'd been secretly seeing and smoking crack with to give me a ride to the airport. I promised him cocaine and sex in exchange for the ride.

I had secretly packed my clothes earlier that night. I knew that if I didn't leave that day, I would never leave. My drugged-up buddy showed up right on time. When we got to the airport, and I walked into the terminal building, I started having second thoughts. I was very high, and I didn't want to get on the plane. All I could think of was calling my buddy and telling him to come back to get me so we could go back to his apartment and keep getting high.

That's when a miracle happened. Just as I was preparing to walk out of the airport, my sister, who had become a flight attendant, appeared seemingly out of nowhere. She later told me the Lord led her to fly to Austin because she knew I was in trouble. There is no telling where I would be or what might have happened to me if I had not gotten on that plane. But as fate would have it, I got on the plane and went to St Petersburg, Florida, to my parents' new home.

CHAPTER 36

IT'S ALWAYS SUNNY IN FLORIDA

When I arrived in Tampa, Florida, I was a complete and utter mess. I feel sorry for my family now for all the pain they must have felt seeing their once happy, smiling, drug-free Christian son getting off a plane looking like a New York City crack whore.

I spent the first week or two at my parents' home in bed, going through withdrawals. It would be fair to say I was a basket case. I cried for days. I couldn't sleep, and I couldn't eat. My mind was a mixture of longings for cocaine, Kevin, and Austin. At the time, I thought I had made a terrible decision by leaving Austin. But then, as the fog began to clear in my head, I began to remember all the terrible things that had happened to me there, not to mention that the drug dealer who had been out to get me was now 1000 miles away. I was in a new place with a chance to start over.

At first, that's exactly what I did. I was in the most beautiful place I'd ever seen at that point in my life. My mother's job had relocated her to Florida as a store manager for Dillard's Department Stores. My parents thus moved to an area of St Petersburg called Tierra Verde. It is a gorgeous little island surrounded by the beautiful blue waters of the Gulf of Mexico – it is something you only see on TV. You have to drive past the golf course and a row of expensive condominiums to get on the island. The homes on the island look like celebrity homes, and the sun is always shining, well, except when it rains.

Again, life made me the luckiest guy in the world, thanks to my loving parents. I do not know what angel dust God poured on my mom and dad when He created them. What I was about to put them through was more than any normal person could take.

I had recovered from my funk and drug withdrawal with a bang. I joined a band out of Tampa called Playpen. They were the complete opposite of what I was about musically. Still, I was desperate to regain my glory as a musician. They were a bunch of half hippie, half college geeks. They all had long hair and wore jeans and white T-shirts. And, of course, they were all straight.

Playpen was a great band, and I had to admit, even as geeky as they were, those boys could play. And that's how they won me over. Imagine me, the goth queen of the universe, singing lead vocals for what I thought was a gay sounding pop band. They were a bunch of pretty boys with no imagination. Their songs were dull and unimaginative, which I hated. Still, as soon I gained their confidence, I started writing the songs and having input on what covers we would play.

Playpen's other thing was the simple fact they were the only band I ever played in that actually got paid to play. We played nearly every week at the local bars, nightclubs, and frat houses around Florida State University. It was 1992, I was 27, and my band was kicking ass and building a huge local fan base.

I found a job waiting tables at a really nice 5-star hotel and restaurant right on the beach. It was a good gig. I took home good money thanks to the many wealthy patrons and celebrities on the grounds and at the bar enjoying the view. I was even making plans to go back to school and finish my degree. Getting my piece of rolled-up paper has always been important to me. It has this air of validation that I constantly longed for in my life. However, soon all hell broke loose.

CHAPTER 37

THE CRACK ATTACK

After work on a very late night, I sat at the bar drinking with my fellow waiters and waitresses. We were pretty drunk, to say the least. I didn't have a car at that time because my car had broken down in Virginia Beach when Kevin and I moved there a few months back. We had made a sad attempt to get away from the bar scene in Austin and the drugs.

Unfortunately, we both hated living in Virginia Beach. Worst of all, my sister and Kevin didn't get along at all. And on top of all that, I started getting migraines from my high-pressure job working as a stockbroker. I loved and hated that job at the brokerage house, but I ended up being fired because a senior broker asked me to pick up some weed for him. He told my boss I was a drug dealer and got me canned.

I was too drunk to ride my bike back home across the bridge, so I asked my buddy if he would give me a ride. I decided to leave my bike at the restaurant and pick it up the next day. It was around four in the morning when we left the restaurant. He said he knew a spot where we could get some crack cocaine. We both had done pretty well tips-wise, so I said, "Sure, why not?"

I had tried crack cocaine previously in Lubbock, during my college year, but it did not affect me. Besides, after watching how my cousin reacted after using the drug, I was turned off by it. A couple of years later, I tried crack again with the Russian guy I saw during one of my famous breakups with Kevin back in Austin. This time it worked, and it worked well. The experience was exciting and somehow helped replace my desire for the needle.

The spot my buddy drove us to was a seedy ghetto neighborhood on the bad side of St Petersburg. When I tell you that I have never been to a scarier, more dangerous place in my life, I mean it! This place was like a desert storm III. The dark streets were lined on both sides with boarded-up houses. Packs of wild black thugs with hoodies roamed the yards, street corners, and yards. Sickly crack whores walking up and down the street from end to end were looking for their next trick and fix.

I'd been in bad neighborhoods before to cop drugs, so I figured there was nothing to be concerned about. In my mind, we would be in and out in a few minutes. But things didn't go that way at all. My buddy located a guy that we thought looked cool, walking down the street. The guy waved at us and gave us a look like he knew what we wanted. We pulled over and rolled down the window. The guy said he had the crack and asked how much we wanted. When my buddy was about to hand the guy the money, out of nowhere, another guy came running over to the passenger side, holding a gun straight to my head.

They took all our money, our wallets, my buddy's wedding ring, and a gold necklace. A week or so later, we went back to that same spot and eventually got the crack we were seeking that night. Smoking that crack took me down a very dark road that I could have never imagined.

Every dime I made from that point on went to buying more crack and finding a place to smoke it. That was the thing about crack. I could do powdered cocaine almost anywhere without being noticed, but the crack is a whole other matter. It requires a 5-inch glass pipe, a lighter, and a bit of steel wool. This probably doesn't seem to be a big deal until you consider that one of the biggest side effects of the drug is extreme, and I mean *extreme*, paranoia! Smoking crack causes you to hear things and even sometimes see things that are not there. You feel like everyone is watching you, especially the cops. And in Tampa, Florida, that was not just paranoia. At that time the area was the murder capital of the United States. The police rained down like stormtroopers on the streets of those poor black neighborhoods.

My new-found crack addiction became my god. Because I lived with my parents, I always had to find somewhere to smoke the crack in relative safety. At first, I went into the nearby woods to smoke, but the paranoia always got the best of me. That's when I decided that the safe thing to do was drive around on the highway back and forth and smoke while driving.

On one of my many binges, I made friends with a couple of local prostitutes who always let me smoke in their 40-dollar-a-night hotel room as long as I kept buying crack for everyone to smoke. One night, in my crack-induced haze, I told the girls I was gay and that I really wanted to meet a guy. They were more than happy to seduce their straight clients, who were also crackheads, to lend me a hand as long as the crack continued to flow.

Before I knew it, it had been almost two weeks since I had blown off my band, and my family had no idea where I was. I lost my job, and everyone was in a panic. As it turned out, while driving all over town looking for me, my mother and father happened to drive by a little seedy hotel after the Lord had told my mother to turn down the street that the hotel was situated on. They turned the corner and recognized the car my father had given me to drive. They pulled into the parking lot and began knocking on every door, looking for me.

Eventually, they reached the room where the three girls and I were in. One of the girls opened the door and spoke to my parents. I was passed out on the bed. I had been up for four or five days. The girls told my parents they were happy they came to pick me up. They said, "Your son is a good kid, and he doesn't belong here with these kinds of people."

After I got home with my parents, I can't tell you the feeling of embarrassment and guilt that smothered me. I felt completely suicidal for the first time in my life. I honestly just wanted to die. My parents prayed and wept and prayed. We must have sat there at that kitchen table for eternity. Well, at least it felt that way to me. I was totally shattered, and worst of all, the prostitutes had taken my last bit of money and my crack.

My parents finally allowed me to go to my room in the basement and sleep. I woke up two days later to my father sitting by my bed. He was just looking at me. I could see he was in deep pain – the kind only a father could feel when he sees his only son throwing his life away. He asked me if I was okay and I said, "No, I'm not." Then he asked me, "Son, what can I do to help you?" I said, "I don't know." The next thing I know, he reaches towards me and hands me the book he was holding. I looked at the title written across the front cover. It was called *Think and Grow Rich*.

My father looked at me and took my hand. He had desperation in his eyes that I had never seen in him before. And then he said something that changed my life. "Son, promise me you will read this book." I looked at him again, and I thought I saw a tear in his eye. I promised him that I would read it.

In the following months, things got much worse. I started stealing money from my parents' account to the tune of $1,500 before they finally noticed the missing money. I stole a car from one of the band members' girlfriend to ride around doing coke with this blond-haired straight boy that I met at the bar one night after a gig. I was pulled over by the police more times than I can remember. I was even attacked by a gang of thugs one night after coming home from a gig while trying to score some crack.

Everything came crashing to a head when I was finally taken to court for pawning a pink Marshall amp that belonged to a girl that I had met. Her name was Mary, and she was the coolest chick I ever met. I actually fell in love with her. We loved the same music, and she had a calming effect on me that I'd never felt before. We tried to have intercourse more than once, but I couldn't give her what she wanted. I was not excited by the female body no matter how much I liked her.

The truth of the matter was that she had told me that I could have the amp. But once we stopped seeing each other, she flipped on me and got really nasty. In the end, my parents had no choice but to hire an attorney to keep me out of jail. The attorney told us point-blank that there was no way I would win if the case went to court. He explained that we were in Pinellas County. She was a young white college student from a rich family in Coral Gables, and I was a black man. It was her word against mine, and I didn't have a chance, especially with my recent drug issues. I pleaded no contest and was sentenced to one year of probation, including community service and random drug testing. I was ordered to pay $900 (the value of the Marshall amp) restitution.

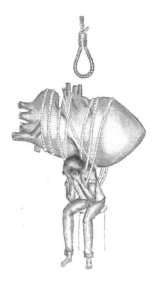

CHAPTER 38

PRAYED STRAIGHT

I kept my promise and read the book my father had given to me. I actually took it very seriously. To sum it up, the book said you have to believe you are already what you want to be. You have to visualize the thing you want in detail with emotion. Basically, you use your imagination to make a thing real to you. The book recommended writing down the thing you want in detail and imagine it as if it were real. So, following the book's directions, I described a day in my music business life.

I imagined myself flying first class to Los Angeles. Then, a black limousine would take me to the record label offices to meet important people and other celebrities and rock stars. I imagined meeting with important people who took me seriously, having dinner at famous restaurants and then ending my evening in a posh Hollywood hotel on Sunset Strip.

After writing my dream down, I took that piece of yellow note paper, folded it up neatly, put it in my wallet, and kept it with me everywhere I went. But there was one more important recommendation the book made. According to *Think and Grow Rich*, the mind doesn't know the difference between fantasy and reality. The way to success is to reprogram the mind. This is best achieved by reading the dream I wrote down every morning when I first woke up and in the evening right before bed. I continued that ritual throughout all the drama and pain I was going through. I read that piece of paper every day, no matter if I was high in a crack trap house in St. Pete or at home in the basement.

At some point, something clicked, and I realized I'd had enough of crack and the whole gay trauma. It seemed like gay relationships were nothing but dirty sex and lies, and that brief time with Mary had given me a look at what life could be like on the other side. I spoke to my parents, and together we decided I should leave Florida and go back to Virginia Beach, where I had friends and support. My sister offered to let me stay with her and her husband.

But before going to my sister's house at the beach, my parents convinced me to go to a Christian rehab. I voluntarily agreed to go. At the time, it seemed like a good idea. I didn't know what to expect or where I was going, but I was mentally and physically shell-shocked by all I'd been through in St Pete, so I just wanted to get as far away from crack as I could.

So, again I packed what was left of my belongings in a small suitcase since everything I owned had either been pawned, sold, or traded for crack. I remember my father taking off work to drive me to the place. It was a farm located somewhere in North Carolina in the middle of nowhere, a few miles from the most redneck town I'd ever seen. The nearest civilization was 75 miles away in Charleston.

To say the place was not what I had expected would be a severe understatement. A collection of small buildings and a ranch-style brick house were situated in the complex center. Behind the house and in every direction there was nothing but woods and open fields. Across from the complex was a stable area with horses and four fat pigs lying about in the mud. There was another smaller building with no windows, just a big cross over the door and a small steeple with a gold cross on top.

After arriving, my father and I were met by a thin elderly white man dressed like a farmer, along with his wife. She, too, was an elderly lady and little plump, naturally friendly, and full of Southern charm and grace. They were very gentle and gave the impression that they really cared about people.

We were given the tour of the grounds, the main house where the farmer/ pastor and his wife lived, the stables, and the dining hall, and the patient housing, which held about 12-15 individuals in shared rooms. I learned that there were a handful of gay people there. They were assigned to rooms that separated them from the straight patients.

After the tour, we sat down in the pastor's office to pray and cast out a few dozen demons that had been possessing me and causing all my problems. After some more praying and calling on the Holy Spirit to set me free, I felt compelled to confess my sins. I told the pastor and his wife that I was gay and wanted to be set free from the life of sin and the devil's power over me. Everyone rejoiced, especially my father, who seemed very pleased at the way things were going. Then we prayed again, and I accepted Jesus into my heart and signed myself into rehab for the next six weeks.

Every day at the rehab was the same. We woke up at 5 am, made our beds, and walked to the dining hall for breakfast. Then we went to Bible study and prayer. Along with all our Bible studies and prayer three times a day, we were also assigned to work either on the farm or off-site. Generally, this meant working as a loader at the local tree mill or working in the fields at one of the other nearby farms.

I stuck to the program, and I gave it my all. I wanted to change. I was desperate for a new life in Jesus Christ, and I prayed as if my life depended on it. I and a couple of the other guys I had made friends with even decided to fast for the last two weeks and ask God to show us himself to be real. Those last two weeks, I drank nothing but water and ate nothing.

On the night before I was to go home, I decided to join my friend, who was also gay, to pray before lights out in the chapel. I remember it well. As I walked into the chapel, I immediately felt the presence of the Lord. His powerful presence led me to the front of the altar. I knelt and began to pray and speak in tongues.

I was immersed in a wave of feelings and emotions. Suddenly, I felt transported out of the chapel, and I was floating in a sea of darkness. The air around me turned ice cold. For a moment, there was only silence. Suddenly I could see my life flashing before my eyes. I began to cry uncontrollably, and I felt overwhelmed by guilt and shame.

But then something extraordinary happened, and I saw a small light like a candle flame that grew and surrounded me. A sea of light flooded me. I felt love like I had never felt before. All my worries and fears melted away, and I was at peace. At some point, I heard a voice and opened my eyes, and there in the flesh was Jesus on the cross, floating above me. He was alive and so real. I could see he was bleeding, and I could see the nails in his hands and feet and the crown of thorns covered in his blood. Tears began to fall down my face like rain, but they were not tears of sorrow or grief but tears of joy.

As I lay there prostrate before my Lord, he lifted his head, looked directly into my eyes, and said, "My child, my son, I know what it is to be a liar. I know what it is like to be a thief. I know what it is to lay with another man. I know what it is to hate oneself. But I died for you, and I created you. You are perfect just as you are. There is nothing to change. I forgive you, now forgive yourself."

I cried and wailed for I don't know how long. Soon, the room began to appear around me again. I was back in the chapel, and I could hear my brothers singing and praising the Lord. It was an experience I'll never forget.

The next day my father and my mother took me to Virginia Beach. For the first time in years, being sober felt great, and I quickly got a job working at a five-star French restaurant. I was making good money, and for the first time, I was saving money. I was amazed by how much money I accumulated so quickly by not drinking and doing drugs. I had joined a church, and I started a Christian band. Although we had a few rehearsals in my sister's garage, we never really clicked, so the band never got off the ground.

Everything seemed to be going great until one day I ran into my old high school buddy, Tony. He asked me to go to the bar with him. At first, I said no. I told him I'd been saved, and I was a Christian. I told him I was no longer gay, nor did I drink or do drugs. I'm not sure how or why, but he convinced me to go anyway. I think I lasted about 30 minutes before I gave in and bought a vodka tonic. After that, all hell broke loose, and before the night was over, we were heading to the hood in Norfolk to buy cocaine.

For the next couple of weeks, I watched my savings disappear as I began doing crack again. When I ran out of money, I started stealing things from my sister's house and pawning them. It wasn't long before everything came to a head, and I decided to end my life once and for all. I couldn't go any further. I'd failed Jesus, my family, and myself. Everything I'd accomplished was wasted. I went to my sister's medicine cabinet and took two bottles or sleeping pills, put on my headphones, lay down on the kitchen floor, and started to drift away. The next day I woke up in the hospital with my mother, my father, my sister, and her husband standing over my hospital bed in tears.

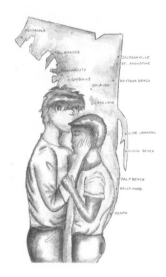

CHAPTER 39

A CHANCE MEETING

My failed attempt at suicide was very hard on my family. I knew I had gone too far. I can only imagine the pain I must have caused them. My parents were clearly shaken and probably at their wit's end. They feared for my life and decided to take me back to St Petersburg with them. I didn't do anything to stop them. I was shaken to my foundation. Everything I wanted to believe in had failed.

When I returned to Florida, I stayed away from the crack by some major miracle and had made a new friend. He was a piano player at the Tierra Verde Yacht Club, who had a thing for me. His name was Scott. He was super nice, an extremely talented, funny, short little guy, who always wore a pair of dark-tinted 70s glasses and sang Billy Joel songs better than Billy Joel. Once I requested "Big Shot," which was my favorite song, and from then on, he sang that song every time I entered the yacht club lounge.

He was always inviting me back to his house for drinks. One night I took him up on his offer. On our way home, we stopped at another local bar. Sitting down on a bar stool, I began to get one of my famous migraines. The loud music was like a hammer to my brain. The pain had become so intense that beads of sweat were running down both sides of my face. I needed to go outside and get some pain pills ASAP. I told Scott I was going across the street to the 7-Eleven to get some Advil.

My migraines were epic. It was literally like a 22.5-magnitude earthquake was going off in my head. Honestly, the pain was beyond description. Years later, I was told by a doctor that I suffered from cluster migraines. They came hard and fast but generally lasted only 30 minutes to an hour.

I didn't know too much about health back then. I took 10, sometimes 15 Advils at a time, desperately trying to stop my pain. It's sort of a euphoric feeling that slows down your face when the tension starts to release, and the pain subsides. I imagine it is what heroin feels like.

As I was walking out the door holding my head in my hand and with my left eye closed shut from the pain, I noticed a guy walking towards me. I smiled and said, "Hello, my name is Houston. I'm from Texas… there are no good-looking men in this town." The guy didn't say anything. He just laughed out loud.

I bought some Advil at the store and sat in my car with the air conditioner on full blast for 10 or 15 minutes until the pain finally subsided, and I slowly started to feel like my sassy self again. I jumped out of the car and walked back into the bar as if nothing had happened. I sat down on the barstool, and there he was: the cute guy I had seen at the door was sitting in the seat next at the bar. I took a quick drink of my vodka, then I turned to face him and started going on about Texas and how much better things were in Austin blah blah blah.

The poor guy must have been bored to death listening to me ramble on. But he just sat there and let me go on till I had to stop to breathe. I guess at some point I took a pause, and that was when he asked me if I played pool. I smiled at him and said yes. And with that, my life took another unexpected turn. I met Kimball, the love of my life.

Kimball was everything and then some, professional, confident, and smart, the perfect husband and an unbelievable cook. He was my greatest mentor, a businessman, a provider, a comforter, a fountain of knowledge, and most of all, he was my best friend. Kim, as I called him, was an attractive, short, slightly plump little bear from Santa Cruz, California. He had dark brown hair and bright hazel eyes, and a charming demeanor that everyone loved. He had a tone in his voice that could charm the scales of a snake. Kim had a passion for life and for a good time. He had impeccable taste and a drive for the good things in life like no one I had ever met.

I wouldn't say it was love at first sight, but it was damn sure close to it. Kim was an impressive man, and everything about him screamed success and class. He had a great ranch-style home on the water, just a few miles from my parents', with a screened-in swimming pool. Beyond the pool was a long wooden pier that led down to the boat dock where Kim's sailboat was anchored.

Kim came into my life at just the right time. He was a breath of fresh air for a recovering drug addict like me. Suddenly I stopped doing drugs. I no longer had any desire or need to use cocaine, weed, or crack. Well, at least not like before.

Kim became my rock, my champion, and my knight in shining armor. He was a liberal Jew and hated seeing anyone's rights violated. And he felt that my family and the Church were violating my rights. He believed people were born gay and that the Church discriminated against gay people unjustly.

Kim immediately took offense to the hostile manner in which certain members of my family treated him. My parents and sister were constantly calling and preaching to me about the life I was choosing to live, and the desperate need to get right with the Lord. Kim always pointed out the radical change in my mood and demeanor every time I interacted with my family. He said I became like a child every time I spoke to them on the phone. I listened to Kim vent his anger and frustration towards my family and how they treated me repeatedly. Most of the time, it would escalate into a fight between him and me, because at first, I defended my family and their beliefs. I was raised to believe in the Bible; I didn't know anything else. However, Kim and I had deep, meaningful conversations, and his insights into human nature always impressed me.

Kim was the first man to show me the finer things in life. We always ate at the best restaurants, drank the best wines, and smoked the finest cigars. He had an excellent taste like no one I'd ever known before. He wore beautiful but manly clothes, finished with a Rolex, and fine tailored shoes and suits. Sometimes he wore his Tag Heuer or his Omega Constellation, depending on the occasion. He drove a two-seater convertible and a company car that he let me drive. But best of all, he had Teddy. Teddy was an adorable black chow who became my adopted "son," who I still miss to this day.

After that chance meeting, I fell deeply in love with Kimball, so much so that I wanted to be like him. I felt like I'd met someone I could trust and look up to. Someone who could show me the way to a better, more successful life. When a month or so later, Kim accepted a job transfer offer to Jacksonville, Florida, to get me as far away as he could from my parents, I was ready to follow him wherever the wind blew.

CHAPTER 40

JEWISH AMERICAN PRINCESS

We settled into a beautiful Tudor-style home in an upscale neighborhood on the westside of Jacksonville. The streets were lined with tall oak and pine trees. Kim taught me the importance of location, location, location, status, and real estate value. The house we rented also had a massive pool and a jacuzzi, which sold me on the place. Kim surrounded us with beautiful things, always the best brands and the latest trends. Kim also loved to throw dinner parties at home and entertain. He was hands down the best cook on earth. His food was and still is the best I've ever tasted. Even food from the best restaurants can't compare.

A couple of days before the move, I finally told my parents I was moving away. They thought I was making a big mistake. They said we wouldn't last two years together, and that Kim was only using me for sex. Kim was 16 years older than me. He was 40 when we met, and I was 24. My parents saw Kim as the devil, viciously preying on their lost and confused son who desperately needed to be saved by Jesus Christ.

To my surprise, a month later, my parents moved into a condo two miles from me and Kim. Apparently, my mother, too, was offered a transfer to be the store manager at the Orange Park Dillard's in Jacksonville. When I told Kim about my parents moving to Orange Park, he laughed for about ten minutes, then said something about my parents staring at us.

For all his wonderful traits, Kim also had a roving eye that was always a threat; I had a hard time trusting him at the beginning of our relationship, and I often became very jealous. I first noticed Kim's infidelity before leaving for Jacksonville when his ex visited us one weekend. I caught Kim and his ex together, half undressed. Of course, Kim denied that anything ever happened. Still, I knew better, and years later, he would finally admit something did happen.

In Jacksonville, I was sitting at home playing housewife for the first few months. I spent my time reading books, arranging the house, and taking care of the dog. My dad came to our house often unannounced to play table tennis in my garage or to give me a new cassette tape or CD on success and top-selling techniques or motivational speaking. My father adored motivational speakers like Anthony Robbins, Myles Monroe, Earl Nightingale, Brian Tracy, and Napoleon Hill. And I soaked it all in like a dry sponge.

He gave me tapes on brain-mind expansion and deep hypnosis for success. He gave me tapes on psycho-cybernetics, the science of the mind, *The 48 Laws of Power*, Machiavellian philosophy, Plato, Marcus Aurelius, the *One Minute Manager*, *Swim with the Sharks*, *The Strangest Secret*, *Rich Dad, Poor Dad*, autobiographies on Einstein, Edison, Tesla, and anything and everything about selling, especially to the rich. And again, I soaked up every drop.

My father had become obsessed with becoming rich ever since he retired from the Navy in 1986. My mother's career had blossomed, and she was the definitive breadwinner. My father was a proud man and believed the man should be the breadwinner.

One time my father told me a salesman could write his own check and get a job anywhere, which turned out to be true most of the time. I knew I could always get a job as a commission salesman whenever I got into a jam and needed fast money or a steady job. I learned that back in Austin, my first time selling cars at Leif Johnson Ford. During my first week at the dealership, I made $1,500 in commissions. Selling cars is how I paid the rent for Kevin and me for 3 years.

I absorbed page after page of success books. I woke up and went to bed listening to subliminal affirmation tapes. I created success journals and made dream boards. I wrote down my goals and visualized myself successfully. I did this ritual every day. Slowly but surely, I started to believe what I was reading.

It is important to mention that with all the business and motivational books I read, I equally devoured hundreds of books, articles, videos, and documentaries on secret societies, ancient cultures, human origins, and the magical arts. It was not unusual to find me engrossed in books like *The Key of Solomon*, *The Book of Enoch*, or studies in the Kabballah, Hinduism, Islam, or the ancient cultures and religions. One might call me a self-taught scholar of world religions and ancient history. To this day, I have an unquenchable thirst for knowledge.

My thought processes and belief patterns were changing dramatically day by day. Funny thing was I wasn't doing drugs at all. I told my parents they had driven me to the brink of suicide with all the guilt they forced on me about being gay, and I told them I didn't have to take it anymore. And through my newly educated eyes, I could see I was right. It was my life, not theirs. Then one day, it all just clicked in my head. I simply started to fake it till I made it. I became the person I wanted to be, not tomorrow or when everything is perfect. I realized NOW was the time. Now is the only time.

I sat down in my home studio and wrote out a plan. Step one: Go back to school and study music. Step two: Get every book I can find on the music business and study it. Step three: Get a job related to music. Step four: Get an internship at a recording studio. Step five: Start a new band.

CHAPTER 41

BACK TO SCHOOL OR BUST

The first few years went by fast in our new city of Jacksonville. I don't think there was or ever has been a happier time in my life. Kim and I were the perfect couple, and we had an amazing new circle of friends.

Unfortunately, during that early period, Kim had been sued by an employee for sexual discrimination. Before that time, Kim was totally in the closet. During the lawsuit, he came out completely to his company to prove his innocence. The whole affair was very messy, but somehow it brought Kim and me closer together. He eventually won the lawsuit.

That same year, Kim was chosen regional manager of the year for Cole National, which came with a huge bonus and a 10-day cruise to the Caribbean, spouse included. Kim bravely told the company that I was his significant other, and we went on one of the best vacations I've ever been on. It was truly magical. Kim surprised me with a beautiful diamond ring on our first night in St Thomas.

The strangest thing was how open and accepting everyone in the company was to me, including the CEO. I had never felt so good about myself. I was clean. I even stopped smoking cigarettes. I wasn't going to bars, bookstores, or gay saunas, and I wasn't cheating on Kim the way I had so shamelessly done with Ben and Kevin.

The boiling tension between my parents and Kim had lowered to a mild simmer. The more positive changes they saw me make, the more they began to accept my relationship. Although there were still moments of discomfort and hostility between Kim and my family, we spent every Christmas and nearly every Thanksgiving holiday together.

The first time I realized that my mother had finally accepted Kim was when she asked him to help her with Christmas dinner. My mother was a finicky eater and rarely ate other people's cooking. Still, she and my family eventually came to love Kim and his cooking.

I was a new man, or as Kim called me, a "Jewish American Princess." He spoiled me, and I believe it gave him great joy seeing me transform from the lost crackhead he met at the bar into a brilliant, motivated, creative person with goals and ambitions. Time and time again, Kim and my father encouraged me to focus on my goals. Between the two of them, I reprogrammed for success.

In the meantime, I enrolled at Florida Community College, majoring in music and minoring in business finance. I worked part-time as assistant manager of the CD Warehouse and part-time intern at Black House University Records.

In my first year back in college, I made nearly perfect grades and even made the Dean's List. All the success books I read told me that I needed to master my craft and gain specialized knowledge. Majoring in music made perfect sense to me and was in harmony with my goals at that time in my life. At work, I was quickly promoted to store manager and given my own store to run. I was very well liked at the recording studio where I interned. Soon, I became close personal friends with the owner and his baby's momma, who also happened to be the studio manager.

I met all kinds of people in the business through my internship at the studio and made amazing contacts. My store was number one in the district, and my customers and my employees loved me. With Kim's mentorship as a successful manager, I quickly became the sales trainer for my district's other stores. I had finally found success in every area of my life at that time. I'd left all the hurt and pain of Austin and St Petersburg behind me. With Kim, it seemed like everything was possible.

Something else happened that made everything complete: Kim bought a house. We had hoped to put both our names on the mortgage. Still, my credit score was so low at that time that putting me on the mortgage was next to impossible without putting more money down and paying a much higher interest rate. In 1994, we moved into a 3000-square-foot home in the beautiful Ortega Farms Circle.

I remember the first time we drove over to see the place. I refused to get out of the car. The place was situated on ¾ of an acre surrounded by thick woods in the back, and on one side, the yard was overgrown, and the place looked like no one had lived there for years. After a heated argument, Kim convinced me to go inside. The place was worse from the inside than the outside. But Kim saw a diamond in the rough. He sold me on the dream, and we bought the house and moved in a few months later.

Everything was great! During my first year back in school, I formed a band that I decided to call Black Betty, after a black hooker in a novel I had read. For the first time in a long time, I was myself again. I was clean and sober, and I was moving towards my dream of being a rock star. I was learning about recording and how the business really worked. The secret I learned was that it was all about relationships. It really *does* matter who you know.

Then the universe decided to throw a monkey wrench into the mix. It started when I was having trouble with one of my classes, and I decided to hire a student tutor on the recommendation of my professor. The tutor was a big guy, at least 6 feet tall, and solid like a bear. We had scheduled a tutoring session and agreed to $25 an hour. On the day of my first lesson, I got a call from one of my employees at my store telling me the person who was supposed to come in had just quit. I could not get anyone to come in and cover the shift, so being the manager, I had no choice but to go to work.

Naturally, I called the tutor and left him a message explaining the situation. I asked if he could reschedule the lesson for another day. The next day at school, as I was walking to my class, I was suddenly confronted by the tutor. He was visibly enraged and looked like I had stolen something from him.

He stepped directly in front of my path. He began accusing me of owing him money for blowing him off with the lesson. I protested and explained that I called him in plenty of time to reschedule the session. I tried my best to remind him we had not agreed that I would pay even if I missed a session. Unfortunately, this enraged him even more. He suddenly began screaming and threatening to beat my black ass with a baseball bat after school if I did not pay him the money that he claimed I owed him. My first reaction was to hit the guy. Still, something about being sober for the past year allowed me the benefit of remaining calm.

After the guy finished threatening me, he walked back into his class, but my blood was still boiling. I wanted to do something about the situation and decided to go to the Dean's office and report the incident. When I got there, I explained the situation as calmly as I could to his secretary, who took my statement and then asked me to go with her to point out the tutor.

This turned out to be a huge mistake. When we got upstairs to his classroom, the tutor was in, and I pointed him out to her. Somehow, he saw us looking through the glass door, and he jumped up out of his seat, stormed out of the class, and punched me in the face. I lost my cool, and without thinking, I quickly pulled out a pair of sharp scissors I had in my bag. Before I could stab him, security came out of nowhere, and I was arrested for assault.

I was accused of being a drug dealer and held on a $50,000 bond. That incident was probably one of the worst experiences of racism that I had ever experienced, even worse than being attacked by the skinheads in Austin. I spent four days in jail, and it cost my parents $8,000 to bail me out. The charges were eventually dropped, but I was suspended from school for one year and given failing grades in all of my classes, even though I had worked so hard. That was the end of that. I never went back to school.

CHAPTER 42

WELCOME TO THE MUSIC BUSINESS

Now that completing my degree was no longer an option, I became horribly bitter for quite a bit of time after being expelled. But despite my sudden academic misfortune, a few months later, fate smiled on me again, and I was offered a job in Clearwater, Florida, to manage corporate sales for a company called Subsonic Distribution.

Clearwater is a four-hour drive from Jacksonville, but Kim decided to take the offer after talking to my mentor. The company had established itself as the #1 distributor of electronic dance music (EDM) to local mom and pop stores across the country. My job was to create the corporate division of the company's distribution arm. I knew nothing about EDM, nor did I care in the least. I was still a goth at heart, but it didn't matter to me as long as it was music related. I knew sales, and everything I had read about success and selling gave me the confidence that I would succeed.

I made a great deal with the company: I would take a salary of $500 a week in return for a commission rate of 5% that would max out at 25% once I reached a certain number in sales, plus a 1% override on my sales team that I would build and train. The one thing I didn't think about was the four-hour drive that I had to make every Monday morning, leaving at 4 am to get to work on time. During the rest of the week, I originally rented a room from an older couple that I honestly could not bear being around. Later I moved into an apartment with the general manager.

The drive was very hard at first, but later I got used to it. I figured out how many CDs I needed to get there. I'd always roll a joint and get high and drive. I sang along to my music of one of my favorite groups, blasting my speakers until I saw the Tampa/Clearwater exit sign.

I also saw the job as my ticket to get my band's music distributed or signed to a major label. I always had big dreams, no matter what job I was doing. Whether I was selling cars or waiting tables, I always saw myself as a musician first, and my "day job" was merely a means to an end.

On my first day, I was given a small desk and a multi-line phone in the main salesroom corner. There were ten other salesmen with stacks of records and CDs on their desks. These guys knew the music and had no problem selling to the company's existing accounts. The top salesman at that time had a desk behind mine. He was doing $25,000 a week in sales and had the big top mom and pop store accounts. These guys were good, but I knew I could be even better.

I knew a good song when I heard it, and I knew how to sell anything to anyone. I sat there day after day using what I had learned from all the books I had read and made as many calls as possible. As we often played a track over the phone for a potential buyer, I would spend hours researching, listening to music, and selecting the very best CDs and vinyl to use for my sales pitches.

In the first month, I didn't sell anything, but I wasn't concerned. I knew selling was a numbers game, and I knew how to win it. I knew that sooner or later the odds would be in my favor and that someone would eventually say yes to me. And that's exactly what happened.

The first account I landed was Virgin Records. At that time, Virgin Records had 19 stores across the US and Canada. The head buyer was a guy named Randy Myers. I called him 25 times before he took my call. Then I called him 35 times before he said yes to me. On that 36th call, Mr. Myers ordered $65,00 in CDs from me. Overnight I became the star of the company.

And as sure as rain in Seattle, soon everyone was talking about Houston, the wizard. Before I knew it, I was selling more than all the other salesmen combined. I was on fire and sometimes making as much as $8,000 a month in salary plus commissions.

Unfortunately, all wasn't gravy in my personal life. The long drive week after week and being away from Kim were taking a toll on me. No matter who I was with, my insecurities about cheating and breaking up followed me, probably because I grew up watching my dad cheating on my mother constantly. Worst of all, I was smoking pot and drinking again, and my demons came back.

One day instead of going to lunch with my colleagues like I normally did, I decided to go somewhere on my own and find a place to eat. I got in the car, rolled a joint, and started to drive. As I passed an adult bookstore, old habits started pulling at me.

I drove by the place a couple of times, trying to make up my mind about going in. My mind was racing with thoughts of guilt and excitement. I knew that if I went into that bookstore, I would cheat on Kim, and I wouldn't be able to take it back. I sat in the parking lot for a minute then looked around to be sure I didn't see any of my colleagues' cars. I went in. From then on, I repeated that ritual almost every day.

All the money I was making I deposited into Kim's bank account. I trusted him with the money to pay our bills. Besides, he was better with money than I ever was. I never questioned him once about where the money was going or what to spend it on.

My success at Subsonic was a double-edged sword. I met real players in the game and attended music conferences like the Ultra Music Festival and the NARM Convention. I dealt with labels from all over the world. I created a division that put the Visiosonic DJ software and Subsonic distribution on the map. On the other side of that sword, my fellow salesman resented my success and were always gunning for me. Besides, the company was going through a changing of the guard.

The CEO and all the executives at Company were Scientologists. My direct supervisor was Vice President Tanya Fisher. She was a very nice lady and very professional. I learned a lot from her about how to be an executive. I learned quickly how to stay in her good graces by simply reading a chapter each night from the book called *Dianetics* by L. Ron Hubbard that she had given me one day seemingly in passing. Each time she came over from our parent company's main Visiosonic building, I would find the right moment in the conversation to tell her something new I'd learned from the book.

Unfortunately, for all her savvy experience and intelligence in business terms, she was completely clueless about the music and the artists and labels we distributed. Without them, we had nothing as far as I was concerned. Being an artist myself, I knew how sensitive artists are about their music and, more importantly, who they choose to trust with that music. Tanya never understood this fact, which one day eventually led her to insult one of the biggest DJ's in the country so much that he pulled his record from our distribution, which ultimately got her fired.

Tanya getting fired left me with a wide-open target for my new boss. She was another female Scientologist executive. She was nothing like Sara, and she didn't like me, and I definitely didn't like her. Something about her just rubbed me the wrong way. I was set for a battle that I was determined to win.

Meanwhile, with each passing day, my guilt and shame grew as I found myself addicted to adult bookstores and getting high every day. I was even going to work high at that point. I thought my shit didn't stink, and I could do anything I wanted. I had the corporate account that brought in all the money. My head had gotten bigger, and I was now doing other drugs and drinking regularly. I know I was self-medicating from the shame and guilt of what I was doing at lunchtime and after work. I was completely addicted to quick and easy anonymous sex.

Every Friday, I would leave work and head back to Jacksonville. Sometimes I would stop at the bookstore, sometimes not, but I always went home with that guilt. I never told anyone, especially not Kim, who I'd always been honest with until that point. I knew in my heart that he could sense something had changed between us. I think we both felt it.

CHAPTER 43

EVERYTHING IS
BETTER IN TOKYO

It was around this time that I was introduced via telephone to a girl named Cyndi Ferguson. Cyndi lived in Japan and came highly recommended as a legit Japanese concert promoter by the studio owner I once interned for in Jacksonville. Over the next few weeks, she and I spoke on the phone. We began to paint a glorious picture of the music opportunities that Japan had to offer. She sold me, hook, line, and sinker. Finally, she made me an offer that I couldn't refuse. That's when I decided to leave Subsonic and started planning my exit strategy.

Cyndi was a tall African American girl. Very smart savvy and she spoke fluent Japanese and Chinese. She was very impressive at first. Over time she convinced me to find an investor and co promote a Hip HOp tour in Japan.

When my new boss had cut my commissions in half, it forced me to put in my two weeks' notice. This happened the same week I discovered the general manager of the distribution division that had hired me was skimming thousands of dollars off the top as well as stealing records and making bad deals with labels that would eventually cripple the company. More and more labels and artists claimed they had not been paid in months for their products.

After a couple of days of researching contracts and invoices, it became clear to me the company was imploding on an irreversible path of bankruptcy. But I wasn't going down with the ship. Without letting anyone, including my personal assistant Lori, know what I was doing, little by little, I began taking my personal files with me and erased the hard drive on my company computer.

Things were so volatile that I nearly got into a fistfight with the general manager, who called me a traitor for exposing his theft. In a way, I did feel guilty for exposing him. After all, he did hire me for the job. But at the same time, I hated him for what he did. He destroyed everything we all worked so hard to achieve with his greed and short-sightedness.

After I left, the distribution arm of the company became unglued. No one knew how to place or fulfill orders. No one even knew who to contact because I'd removed all of my files.

I was glad to be rid of the endless 4-hour drive, and now that I was away from the bookstores, my life at home was better. I put it in the back of me and locked the door.

Cyndi and I continued to talk, and in a few weeks, we devised a plan to produce concerts at Tokyo's best venues bringing artists like Eve, Ja Rule, and Redman. The plans she laid out were so detailed, and she was smart and effective at selling me the dream. I also saw this opportunity as a way to promote my band. I had the connections, and I knew I could make the deal. All we needed was $90,000 to pay the down payments on the artists and the venue. And I knew where to get it.

I had taken kung fu classes for a brief time from a Chinese doctor by the name of Mr. Chow. During that period, Mr. Chow and I had several conversations about my job, the music business, and his interest in concert promotions. He told me he had access to funding from China and his import-export business. I knew he was my guy. I made an appointment to meet with him and explained the plan. He was interested but had a million and one questions. We had meeting after meeting as well as phone calls to Japan with Cyndi. Finally, an agreement was made between Cyndi and

Mr. Chow: I would travel to Japan, meet Cyndi, review the team Cyndi had claimed to oversee, and simply give the deal the stamp of approval.

It was about this time that the Internet was coming alive. I had found a site called bear411.com, and I discovered there were bears all over the world. I started corresponding with guys all over. In the back of my mind, I had thoughts of meeting one of those bears in Tokyo. Life with Kim started to feel mundane.

Our sex life had become, frankly, boring and routine and had left me feeling unfulfilled. At the time, I didn't know Kim was feeling the same way. I began to dream of meeting a new man. As much as I loved Kim, physically he was no longer what I was attracted to. To add to our problems, Kim was versatile and longed for something that I couldn't give him. Nevertheless, he supported me 100% and even advised me throughout the deal.

We set the date a week later for my flight to Japan, and I had to rush to get my passport expedited. I said goodbye to Kim once again and flew off to the land of the rising sun. I arrived in Japan on a high note. Cyndi was the perfect hostess. She introduced me to the Who's Who of the Tokyo hip hop scene. I met the best DJs, promoters, and label heads. I even went in the studio with top J-pop acts and the legendary DJ Yutaka, known across Japan as the father of Japanese hip hop.

But then, the night before I was to return to America, something extraordinary happened. Dan, the program director from Tokyo's number one radio station 76.1, asked me to meet him for a drink. Cyndi had always been with me, but that night she left me at her apartment to run some errands.

I met Dan a few blocks away at one of the local bars. At first, Dan was meticulous in choosing his words, but as we continued to speak, we both slowly realized some serious issues with Cyndi's master plan. Dan didn't fully trust her and urged me not to send the money directly to Cyndi but to put it in an escrow account until we were all certain of who she really was.

He had only known Cyndi for a short time. She was an American that had appeared on the Tokyo hip hop scene virtually overnight. She introduced herself as a high-level promoter from the States. She said she came to town to set up an office in the high-end business district in Tokyo. She was flashing money and dropping big American names all over town. Of course, everyone wanted to be involved in her big ideas to bridge American and Japanese hip hop.

When I got back to Cyndi's place, I thought about everything Dan and I had discussed. The thing that stood out the most to me was that Cyndi had told everyone I was staying at the Hyatt in Shinjuku. Instead, the truth was I had been sleeping on her couch for the past week. I needed to make a decision.

I sent Mr. Chow an email telling him everything looked good, but I still had some questions that needed to be answered. I further admonished Mr. Chow not to send the funds directly to Cyndi, just as Darryl had recommended. As I couldn't get my laptop to connect to the Internet, I had to send the email on Cyndi's laptop.

The next morning Cyndi dropped me off at the airport. She was all smiles and kisses. We couldn't wait to get the ball rolling. Fourteen hours later, when I arrived back in Jacksonville, Kim was waiting for me, saying that Mr. Chow had requested that we meet as soon as I returned. Mr. Chow came to the house that evening, and he, Kim, and I sat in the dining room as we had done several times a week for the last month or so, and I was handed the shock of the century.

As I sat there listening, Mr. Chow explained how I was no longer a part of the Japanese deal. I think I sank into a momentary coma as I slumped over the impressive oak wood dining table in shock – the very table we shook hands and declared our honorable partnership. I was speechless. So much for the honor and loyalty bullshit I heard when we started.

Mr. Chow further explained that Cyndi had read my email and sent Mr. Chow her version of the story. She painted me as an unfocused partier that went out and got drunk every night. It was partly true because I did go out with the radio crew to either a party or event every night to network.

However, it wasn't all bad news. Mr. Chow promised to give me a finder's $10,000 for my time and the opportunity I created for him and his Chinese partners who provided the 90,000 dollars. Also, the word got around quickly in the Florida music scene about my recent exploits in Japan, and I began receiving call after call from artists and labels to get their records into the Japanese market.

About a month later, I received a call from Mr. Chow. My first thought was to tell him to go fuck himself, but I was too curious to hear what he had to say. We met again at my house and sat around the dining room table. Mr. Chow's normal calm exterior was visibly disturbed. I'd never seen him, the martial arts master, look so out of sorts. I saw fear in his eyes as he explained to me how a week after sending Cyndi the $90,000, all communication stopped, and the money was gone.

This revelation did not shock me, as I had warned him not to send Cyndi the money. It was what he said next that not only terrified me but poor Kim as well. Out of nowhere, Mr. Chow revealed that the money had come from the Chinese Mafia. For those of you reading that aren't familiar with the Chinese Mafia, let me put it to you the same way Mr. Chow explained the situation to me. "The Chinese Mafia does not take losses."

Mr. Chow said that the Chinese Mafia was looking for Cyndi and would deal with her and anyone else involved in their traditional fashion. To my relief, he told me that they had given me a pass since I had originally warned them of my concerns. However, for months after that meeting, I was living in complete fear and paranoia. I kept expecting ninjas dressed in all black to appear out of the shadows and strangle me or cut my head off. The smoke did finally clear, and my fears of being murdered subsided just as they had done in Austin when I feared for my life from the psycho drug dealer that I owed money. But the whole affair left a nasty taste in Kim's mouth.

A few weeks later, I got a call from Patrick, the owner of one of the labels I distributed. He wanted to know if I could meet him for lunch, and I accepted. We met in Tampa at a local restaurant. He told me he'd seen my success at Subsonic and wanted to hire me as a consultant to help him get his CDs in stores directly from his label. I still had good connections, and this was in alignment with everything I had learned from my studies and my new bible, *Think and Grow Rich*.

I accepted his offer and set out to attend every music business convention I could get to. I arrived at each event armed with business cards and pamphlets about me and my services as a music business consultant. Just like in that lame Kevin Costner movie, *Field of Dreams*, I built it, and they came. Before I knew it, I began to receive calls from labels across the country. This is how I got in touch with a guy named Klaus, who was a former producer of a legendary boy band.

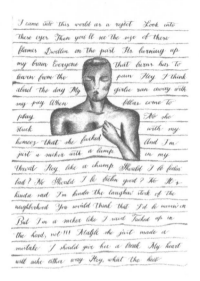

CHAPTER 44

MAKING THE BAND

I turned 35 at the beginning of the new millennium when I took a new job as Marketing Director for a major studio. located in Sanford, Florida, which is a small affluent area of beautiful Orlando. It was a dream job for a guy like me at the time. I gained access to people and places in the industry I could never have dreamed of before.

I returned to Japan, and I strengthened the alliances I had made over there previously as well as sharpened my skills as a promoter and industry tastemaker. I attended the Billboard Hip Hop Awards under the direction of the label's publicist. She had even set up a private meeting with the then legendary Ted "Bet on Ted" Mac, who was known from coast to coast as the king of rap promoters.

Ted's title at the time was Senior VP of the Rap Department of a major independent record label. Hip hop had begun to rule the radio airwaves in the late 1990s and early 2000s with artists like 50 Cent, G Unit, Eminem, Keshia Cole, and The Game. Ted had made an early name for himself based on his ability to get the streets behind a record.

We wanted Mr. Mac's magic touch, aka his street teams, to break our artist. However, the meeting our publicist set up for us didn't go quite the way we planned.

We met in a private suite that had been set up for independent labels and artists to meet and greet with Mr. Mac and his team from the Interscope Rap Department. The room was full, and people were coming in and out. There were bottles of booze, mainly Hennessy and trendy brands of vodka, being offered as hospitality. We were all dressed to the nines, wearing designer outfits, expensive watches, and shoes. Mr. Mac, however, was surprisingly dressed in an old white T-shirt and sweatpants. He didn't even wear a watch. He weighed at least 450 lbs, and he was the loudest person in any room. He was larger than life, literally, and I was fascinated instantly. I knew right then and there that I had to work with him. He was everything I wanted to be. He was confident, savvy, and didn't give fuck about what anyone thought of him.

I guess the best way to describe the very, VERY short meeting would be to compare it to the movie, *Clash of the Titans*. Super producer vs Super record promoter, like most of the people in the industry, both had massive, supernova-size egos. So, after Mr. Mac finished listening to the tracks we played him, he proceeded to tell The Viking none of the songs were urban enough for radio, nor were there any hits. Klaus looked at Mr Mac and calmly reminded him he had sold 70 million records. Mr. Mac responded that he didn't give a fuck about how many records he had sold. The two of them began shouting, and before we knew it, we were being escorted out of the suite.

It all happened so fast that my main concern was how to get Mr. Mac's number. Going into the meeting, our publicist, Yasmine, had told me the importance of networking and making as many connections as possible, and taking full advantage of the opportunity to attend the Billboard Hip Hop Awards. I took her advice seriously.

As we came out of the elevators into the beautiful main lobby of the famous Fontainebleau Hotel, I saw an ATM, and I suddenly remembered something that I learned from Cyndi Ferguson back in Japan. I went to the ATM, withdrew my limit, and headed back to the elevator to Mr. Mac's suite. I had no idea if he would even still be in the room, or if he would let me back in the room at all. But as fate would have it, the room was empty except for Mr. Mac and our publicist, Wendy, who had stayed behind when Klaus stormed out.

Wendy took the liberty to walk me over to Mr. Mac and make the introduction. When Mr. Mac reached out his hand to shake mine, I transferred the hundred-dollar bills that I had cupped in the palm of my hand into Mr. Mac's hand. The transfer went as smoothly as any drug deal I had done at the gay bars back in Texas. Mr. Mac slowly released my hand, and I watched as he quickly glanced at the money. He stuffed the hundred-dollar bills into his pocket, smiled at me, and said, "I like the way you get down, Houston. Fuck that white boy." A few months later, Klaus's project derailed. Things just don't always work, no matter how good the music or the team is. That's what makes the music business so exciting because you never know when a song will sink or sail.

I spent the next few days following Mr. Mac everywhere. He was a tour de force. Everyone wanted to be near him. Everywhere he went, a crowd would form, and one after the other, artists and executives would come to shake his hand or buy him a drink and pay tribute to him.

I was given Mr. Mac's personal cell number. At the time, I did not realize how much of an honor that was. I had been chosen to enter into an elite circle that I never knew had existed, and being a member was like winning the lottery. It would be nearly a year later before I would see Mr. Mac again, but I called him often enough to keep my name in his mind, and it eventually paid off.

The studio in Florida was basically the first real pro-level studio I had been to. I was intoxicated by the lights and the gear, the magic that is the art of recording. I was constantly wondering how I could record in a studio like this. But more importantly, I wanted to know how to record like Herr Klaus. I knew if he could do it, so could I, and that's when I decided to go back to school for audio recording.

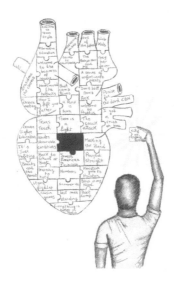

CHAPTER 45

CITY OF ANGELS

I enrolled at ARTI Audio Recording Technology Institute in Orlando. In the beginning, I was driving two hours a day from Jacksonville to Orlando to get to school but eventually found a cheap place with a room to rent. I was a straight-A student and top of my class, which was great on the surface, but I had begun stopping at adult bookstores again. Little by little, I could feel my infidelity affecting my attitude towards Kim. The rift in our relationship continued to expand.

I enjoyed all that I was learning about recording and the gear I had pondered over ever since I purchased my first four-track recorder in 1988. I had recorded before, but the result always sounded like shit to everyone

I played them, well, except for me, of course. I had decided that if I could learn to record, I could make a hit record. However, two weeks before graduation, something extraordinary happened once again.

I was sitting at my desk waiting for class to start, shooting the shit with one of my classmates as usual, when my phone rang. It was Howard, the owner of Blackhouse Records, where I had done my first internship in Jacksonville. He told me he had someone by the name of Keith who wanted to speak to me. He said he had told Keith about my experience in distribution and Japan. More importantly, he told Keith that I knew Kevin Black and could actually get him on the phone. After a brief telephone conversation, I agreed to drive to the studio when I returned home that weekend.

When I got to the studio, I didn't only meet Keith but also someone else. His name was Ron Lotto and apparently, he was the drummer for the biggest band in the world at that time. I was blown away.

By chance, while I was still attending Florida Community College, I had the unpleasant pleasure of interacting with a fellow student about the music business during a class I took on audio production. The classmate in question was a fellow named Ted Hurst. At the time, I had no idea who he was, but I can remember him asking me if I heard of his band. I told him, "No, I'd never heard of them." He rather arrogantly replied, "You will!"

After Keith introduced us, John asked me if I knew who he was. I said no, then he asked me if I knew his band. I said, "Yes, but I am not too fond of your music." Finally, he asked me if I knew Ted Mac, and I said yes. While the guy was still going on about the great band, I dialed Mr. Mac's number.

Mr. Mac and I were on a first-name basis at that point, so when he answered, I greeted him, and then I said, "Kevin, meet my new boss. I handed him my phone and they spoke very quickly for about 30 seconds and, hung up and said, "You're hired."

The new job meant I would have to go to LA. That night I told Kim the good and the bad news. Kim assured me he was one hundred percent behind me. He even went on to tell me that he had already had a successful career, so it was my time to shine.

Days later, I found myself flying first class to LAX to meet the band at their rehearsal space near the famous round Capitol Records building. When I landed, I nearly floated across the LAX concourse. I was starting 2003 off with a major bang!

I can remember that first day in LA as well as I can remember my name. After deboarding the plane, I was greeted by a man dressed in a black suit holding a sign with "Mr. Houston" written on it. The funny thing was when the driver reached down to take my bags, I jerked back in a defensive posture. I could see the man suddenly realized he was dealing with a first-class travel virgin. After he assured me that he was not trying to rob me, I let him take my bags and followed him to the car. The car was a black stretch Mercedes Benz.

Before heading to the studio, the driver took me to Ron's apartment at Marina Del Rey in an ultra-posh apartment building with a list of tenants that read like a celebrity roll call. John wasn't there, but I was greeted at the apartment by Keith, the label's general manager. We got high while the driver sat downstairs for a good hour waiting for us to come down. Then we spent the rest of the day going from one meeting to the next. I was feeling great. I met more important people in the business that day than I ever imagined.

I had been to LA and Interscope Records once before to go to an event with Mr. Mac. That was also the trip where I asked Mr. Mac for a job at the label. He denied my request but told me he would do me a favor and make me an indie. That way, I could work for him without having to live in LA. But being in LA with one of the biggest rock bands in the world at that time was on a whole other level. I would be meeting one star after the other at this studio or that rehearsal space.

Later that evening, we went to a hotel called La Montrose in West Hollywood. instructed me to hurry up and get dressed because we were going to dinner. As I headed to my room to change, I walked through a sea of major stars all standing around chatting about the business in some form or another. I learned very quickly, everything in business is about money. If you are not talking about business or money, no one wants to listen to you for very long.

When I entered my room, I was completely blown away by the opulence. It was by far the nicest, most posh hotel room I'd ever stayed in. I stood there and looked around for a few moments taking it all in. I just reflected on how incredible the day had been and how the people I had met all took me seriously all of a sudden. I felt important.

I took a quick hot shower in the luxury bathroom. I got dressed in a new black Armani suit and Kim's Omega Constellation gold watch. Kim always told me the first impression is the one that counts. I looked in the mirror, and I knew I looked good. I had about 10 minutes before I had to go back downstairs and meet John and Koran in the lobby. So, I decided to kill time by smoking a cigarette.

I had quit smoking for the past year, but constant feuding with Kim about him smoking in the house finally caused me to cave in and start smoking again. I figured if I couldn't beat him, then I might as well join him and stop the routine of him smoking and me bitching about the smell.

I walked out of the gorgeous room onto the small balcony overlooking the Strip, and suddenly my eyes were filled with tears that poured down my face. I pulled the small razor phone from my pocket and dialed my father. When he answered the phone, I shouted into the phone at the top of my lungs, "OMG! Daddy, it worked! It worked! It worked!" Indeed, it had worked. It was the magic of believing, despite my circumstances, that I would succeed. I had been following the instructions of *Think and Grow Rich* to the letter for nearly eight years.

I hung up with my father, and I pulled a little, raggedy yellow piece of paper from my wallet and read it out loud for one last time. I cried and cried. I was happier than I had ever been in my life. I had made it through all the trials and the heartache of disappointment and failure. I had made it through it and came out on top. That night it all came true just as I had written it down on that piece of paper while I was still high on crack eight years ago.

The principles of Mr. Napoleon Hill were simple and consisted of 13 clear and concise steps to follow:

1. Desire- I succeeded because I had a burning desire to be in the music business above all else.

2. Faith- I succeeded because I knew without a doubt that I belonged in the business of music. "The best way to guard against being overwhelmed by failure is to discipline the mind to meet failure before it arrives."

3. Auto-suggestion- I succeed because every day, I told myself I was a music business pro, even when I didn't have a clue what I was

doing. "If you do not see great riches in your imagination, you will never see them in your bank balance."

4. Specialized knowledge- I succeeded because I went back to school and studied music. I read every book I could find on the music business and worked in specialized jobs directly related to music and saw those jobs as training grounds. "No man [...] grows rich on what he calls general knowledge." Specialized knowledge is "the actual knowledge necessary to fill a niche. That knowledge must be somehow acquired and organized."

5. Imagination- I succeeded despite the odds because I constantly imagined myself in the music business. I saw myself as the person I wanted to be. "It has been said that man can create anything which he can imagine."

6. Organized planning- I succeeded because I used organized planning to think my way into the music, attend every event, and meet the right people. "You are engaged in an undertaking of major importance to you. To be sure of success, you must have faultless plans."

7. Decision- I succeeded because I knew without a doubt what I wanted, and I made every decision based on the fulfillment of my burning desire to be in the music business. "The world has the habit of making room for the man whose words and actions show that he knows where he is going."

8. Persistence- I succeeded because I persisted and never gave up despite every setback and deal gone bad. "A definite purpose backed by a burning desire for its fulfillment" is "a definite plan."

9. Mastermind- I succeeded because I systematically surrounded myself with people smarter than me, like my mother, my father, Mr. Black, and Kimball Guilford, who advised me every step of the way. "Coordination of knowledge and effort, in a spirit of harmony, between two or more people, for the attainment of a definite purpose."

10. Sex transmutation- I succeeded because I channeled my creative sexual energy towards making music and studying the business of music. "The emotion of sex contains the secret of creative ability."

11. The brain- I succeeded because I focused my thoughts on music and became in tune with that frequency. "Vibrations are picked up from the ether," and we may all make our own signals stronger through positive emotion.

12. The sixth sense- I succeeded because I followed my instincts. "The medium of contact between the finite mind of man and Infinite Intelligence" and "the point at which the mind of man contacts the Universal Mind."

So now you know my tale. Ask yourself, "Does Houston have a problem, or did he miraculously beat the odds?" Circumstances are not always under our control in this world, but our belief creates the impossible. I believe if

I could achieve my goals under my circumstances, you can achieve your dreams too.

I guess you could say I beat the odds that time. But my problems were just beginning, and again I would tempt fate. I would soon find myself alone, homeless, and sleeping on a futon in a trailer park somewhere in North Carolina. I would have to learn many more lessons before I saw the light and began the process of dying to myself and serving the Creator and all humanity. I look forward to sharing those lessons and experiences with you in my next book.

So, as you put this book down and ponder my story, my dear reader, let me share one last thing that I have come to realize about life: Life is what you make it moment by precious moment. Every day, ask yourself, "What actions have I succeeded in taking that would push me one step closer to my dreams?" Though it may be cliché, always follow your dreams to the highest highs and the lowest lows. It is the Creator who put that desire in your heart. The Creator desires to express Himself through you and fill you with boundless joy in the process.

EPILOGUE

A child molester is an expert at making a child feel like they care for them or make them feel like what they are doing is normal behavior. Child molesters will often attempt to make their victims believe what is happening is their fault.

I ran into one of the Navy officers who had molested me more times than I can remember in the locker room and the bathroom stalls. I was at a bar hanging out with friends, and I recognized his face instantly. Strangely enough, my first reaction was attraction, then anger, then curiosity. I saw that he was alone, so I left my friends and sat down next to the man. I said hello and asked if he remembered me.

He looked at me and said he wasn't sure. I reminded him of what we did in the locker room at the gym, and he suddenly remembered. He told me he was now married and had two boys. I asked him how he felt about having had sex with me when I was the same age as his youngest son. He replied by saying I must have come on to him. I was shocked but not as upset as when he started telling me that his wife was out of town with the kids, and he wanted to know if I'd like to go back to his place.

I literally didn't know what to say. I sat there for a few more minutes and silently cried inside. Then I went back over to my friends, and for a moment, I felt my stomach turning. I felt sick. But then I blinked my eyes and shook my head from side to side. And as I looked at my friends laughing and drinking, somehow, I blocked out what I was feeling and never thought about him again, well, at least until now.

So how does my story end? Certainly not back in 2004. God willing, it's only just beginning. Like they say, "It's not over till the fat lady sings," and I'm definitely not in the mood to sing.

Saint Andrews

Coming Soon:

Book 2

Houston, We Have A Problem... When All Hell Broke Loose

Lightning Source UK Ltd.
Milton Keynes UK
UKHW010638160621
385607UK00001B/22

9 781665 590037